IMELDA FOLEY was born in Derry and educated at Queen's University Belfast, and Trinity College, Dublin where she gained a Ph.D in Theatre Studies from the Samuel Beckett Centre. She was producer of the award-winning Ulster Youth Theatre from 1987 to 1996 and has worked for most of her professional life with the Arts Council of Northern Ireland as Dram͏ ͏ ͏ ͏ ͏ ͏ ͏r. She is a freelance arts consultant and thea͏

the girls in the big picture

Gender in Contemporary Ulster Theatre

IMELDA FOLEY

THE
BLACKSTAFF
PRESS

BELFAST

The author and publisher would like to thank Marie Jones, Christina Reid, Anne Devlin and
Frank McGuinness for the time they gave to be interviewed for this book.
Thanks also go to the writers, poets and dramatists who have allowed extracts of their work
to be included in this publication. St John Ervine's work appears courtesy of his Estate
as represented by the Society of Authors.

First published in 2003 by
The Blackstaff Press Limited
4c Heron Wharf, Sydenham Business Park
Belfast BT3 9LE
with the assistance of
the Arts Council of Northern Ireland

Typeset by Techniset Typesetters, Newton-le-Willows, Merseyside

Printed in Ireland by ColourBooks Limited

A CIP catalogue record for this book
is available from the British Library

ISBN 0-85640-715-1

www.blackstaffpress.com

For my daughter
Anna Rebecca Foley Simmons

Contents

Acknowledgements

My deep and sincere gratitude is to the playwrights, performers and artistic teams whose work has given so much pleasure in so many productions over the years, and so much to think about in the writing of this book. I have been lucky in seeing most of the contemporary work in first production.

My sincere thanks are to my PhD supervisor, Dr Brian Singleton, Trinity College Dublin. His exactitude and intellectual guidance have been constant. Also at Trinity, Dr Anna McMullan has been a source of inspiration and support.

I wish to thank the staff of the Linen Hall Library, Belfast, and most of all Ophelia Byrne, curator of the Theatre and Performing Arts Archive, for her efficiency, knowledge and editorial advice. At a time when Ophelia was completing the *State of Play* exhibition and organising public events surrounding it, she sat up late at night reading my draft and provided valuable notes which informed the editing process.

The Main Library and the Special Collections at Queen's University Belfast have been constant resources and my thanks are due to the staff there. At the Omagh Library, I thank Anne Duffy for her assistance with the Alice Milligan archive.

Judy Friel and Aideen Howard at the Abbey Theatre, Dublin, have forwarded scripts and reviews, for which I am grateful. Marie Jones has also supplied typescripts of her work. Playwrights Anne Devlin, Marie Jones, Frank McGuinness and Christina Reid agreed to be interviewed and I am in debt to them for their time and such lovely friendship. At the Arts Council of Northern Ireland I thank my former and current chief executives, Brian Ferran and Roisín McDonough, as well as my office 'inmates', Pam Smith and Martin Dowling.

For technical assistance, thanks are due to Anne Campbell for her invaluable expertise in formatting draft material. To Maeve Corr for her patience and assistance in drawing up the bibliography, and to Michael Alcorn and Ken Bartley, who solved computer crises, my appreciation. I also thank my brother, Michael Foley, for his fine-tuned literary instincts in dealing with material new to him. Most of all, editor Hilary Bell, Blackstaff Press managing director, Anne Tannahill, and Julie Trouton and Bronagh McVeigh are to be thanked.

I am deeply indebted to Kim Turtle, Nick Hanna and Nora Greer, who provided so much encouragement and domestic help along the way.

To my daughter, Anna, whose teenage life was thrown into premature independence, all my love and thanks. This work is dedicated to her.

IMELDA FOLEY

BELFAST, 2003

Introduction

And the profiled basalt maintains its stare
South: proud, protestant and northern and male
Adam untouched by the shock of gender

Seamus Heaney, 'The Betrothal of Cave Hill'[1]

In 1972 Sam Hanna Bell published *The Theatre in Ulster*, an account of developments from the beginning of the twentieth century. Since then there has not been a dedicated volume addressing or analysing the broad body of work which has, on stage, represented, interrogated and even prefigured the complex condition of Northern Ireland from the 1970s to the present. Recent critical publications on Irish theatre are tainted by a sort of partition phobia and generally include a statutory chapter on the North as an apologetic appendix to the major work. In this context, the establishment of the Linen Hall Library's Theatre and Performing Arts Archive has already made and will continue to make a substantial impact in attracting researchers and fostering analysis.

As international critics and academics have flown in to the North to research and deconstruct Field Day Theatre's ventures of the 19080s, a veritable cottage industry has developed, based on the company's sophisticated articulation of political and cultural aspirations and subsequent representation in the plays it has produced. Its introduction of the concept of the 'fifth province of the imagination', within which oppositional factions might coalesce and old hegemonies dissolve, seemed a positive, even radical, politic in the 1980s and one which is pursued today and articulated in the new Northern Ireland Assembly's *Programme for Government* (2000). Clearing the cultural terrain and creating space for radical thought in Northern Ireland brought on Field Day and its founders, Brian Friel and Stephen Rea, a barrage of labels and branding. But the inaugural production of Brian Friel's *Translations* will survive as a classic, and demonstrates the quarrel between tradition and new values, the need to revise and to invent. The important work of Field Day and playwright Brian Friel, however, has been thoroughly analysed elsewhere and is not the subject of this book.

Cohabiting the big picture of Ulster theatre at that time was Charabanc Theatre Company, founded in 1983 by five actresses who were disillusioned by the prospects which mainstream theatre, such as it was, offered. There is a wealth of journalistic writing on Charabanc and a dearth of critical analysis. The company and its writer, Marie Jones, provide the title for this book and have prompted the initiative which has informed this project.[2] A full history and critical analysis of Charabanc are to be published by American critic Claudia Harris, who has followed the company's work from its inception. This may redress the current imbalance in published criticism of Field Day and Charabanc.

We also await publication of a discrete work on Ulster theatre which focuses on representations of the conflict in Northern Ireland. Lionel Pilkington of the University of Galway proposes a book which dissects and interprets playwrights' responses to the political situation in Northern Ireland over thirty years. Sam McCready, a former artistic director with the Lyric Theatre, Belfast, now living in the United States, is working on a history of theatre in Ulster. In the meantime Ophelia Byrne, archivist of the Linen Hall Library's increasing collection, has produced a valuable short history, *The Stage in Ulster from the Eighteenth Century*. In addition, she has compiled *State of Play*, a self-standing book and catalogue accompanying an important exhibition of seminal twentieth-century productions which have had a theatrical and cultural impact on Ulster society.

So, awaiting these publications, *The Girls in the Big Picture* is neither a history nor a socio-political documentary of Ulster theatre. However, both discourses are employed to examine issues of gender in a context of more familiar issues relating to Northern Ireland – colonialism and sectarianism. The latter is firmly addressed by the Northern Ireland Assembly's *Programme for Government* (2000), with the concept of cultural diversity being paramount. This apparently progressive framework of governmental determinism echoes loudly the ideologies of inclusivity and pluralism promoted by the founders of the Ulster Literary Theatre (ULT) in 1902, and by Field Day and Charabanc in the 1980s.

Subsequently, the women playwrights Anne Devlin, Christina Reid and Marie Jones have in their work presented the deficits of old hegemonies, while prefiguring new ideologies. Without publishing manifestos, they allow the plays themselves to operate. The espousal of pluralism and diversity is central to their work. Playwright Frank McGuinness creates a hybrid culture from fixed identities which can no longer make sense of, or properly inform, new life, whether located in Northern Ireland or elsewhere. His plays construct expedient meta-communities because the real ones are beyond comprehension. It may seem odd to include a male playwright in a volume entitled *The Girls in the Big Picture*, but the interview with McGuinness (see Chapter 6) marks his own insistence on inclusion. In terms of gender, he says, 'I feel no need to vindicate my inclusion in *The Girls*, but I think it would be strange if my work were not in it.'

In a similar vein, Seamus Heaney's lines, with which I open this introduction, suggest an appropriate interpretation of gender which is not simply dictated by biological sex, the binary opposites of male/female. For Heaney, Belfast's imposing Cave Hill is masculine, overpowering, dictatorially omnipresent – a symbol of Ulster, 'untouched by the shock of gender'. Gender here encompasses the attributes and behaviours which create and define culture. The permutations of gender, socio-political as well as historical, must be confronted if Northern Ireland is to move on, rather than reverting to the pre-conflict backwater of quiet bigotry and superficial respectability. This dominant culture, enshrined by Catholic and Protestant alike in the small houses and housing estates of segregated urban districts or the more affluent homes of North Down and further afield, is challenged principally by women writers who can no longer exist within its orbit. They break the silence, their voices interrogating tradition to introduce possibilities that are positively based on feminisation rather than negative values of 'de-masculation'.

The concept of 'the feminine' is not the prerogative of the female. The terminology embraces the old school of the Enlightenment, invokes future possibilities and suggests fluidity, the antithesis of Ulster's 'proud stare'. Hesitance and uncertainty are granted credence beyond the simple stock responses of the affirmative and the negative. There is an important cultural-political debate which must occur in the vast space between 'yes' and 'no' where legitimate compromises replace traditional assertions. A current example of how in Northern Ireland imagery and binary notions of cultural politics continue to influence is in the media's presentation of the Imagine Belfast campaign to bid for European City of Culture, 2008. The idea is essentially feminine: to even begin to think of Belfast transforming into a city of culture is a leap of faith. While there is a healthy undercutting note in the title, the genuine notion of beginning to *imagine* is a positive one which should be developed even though the bid was unsuccessful. *Winning* is a masculine construct. In the attempt to imagine, a feminine concept, the media hauls back to old formulas with panels and pages dedicated to the binary opposites of *for* and *against*, appropriately imaged by harp and Lambeg drum. Again, there is little room for valid uncertainty or interrogation, for *imagining*. In Northern Ireland, contradictions between the value assumptions of stated objectives and their actual practice are borne out daily. A clear example of the true Ulster dictate which negates imagination was an old patriarchy within the 1994 Northern Ireland Forum for Peace and Reconciliation, unable to disguise itself as the female members were told to 'go home and make the tea'.[3]

None the less, a feminine voice has been central to the work of some of our playwrights, who, during the last decades, have consistently prefigured the new image of politics in Northern Ireland. As this has not always been enacted, the feminine voice in theatre has also been drowned out by the din of more commercial and less threatening fare. Marie Jones is the obvious exception. She presents the recognisable stereotypes of Ulster comedy and employs the genre with stunning sophistication to interrogate cultural assumptions and provide alternatives. Christina Reid challenges the fixed masculine security of the backward gaze, to the Somme and to the Boyne. While tradition deserves respect, its values must be interrogated in order to imagine new futures where diversity becomes a strength rather than a source of conflict. Similarly, Anne Devlin's scrutiny of a republican ideology which subjugates women and sanctifies martyrs in the name of freedom creates a broad template for social change. The work of these women writers comprises the central chapters of this book and is framed by a contextual analysis of the ULT and a final chapter on the work of Frank McGuinness.

The pre-partition term 'Ulster theatre' derives from the production of local work by local actors in the early years of the twentieth century, when the ULT was founded to promote the ideology of the Protestant National Association, an alignment difficult to imagine today. However, the terminology still defines the regional and, perhaps, the political context of theatre in Northern Ireland. Chapter 1 outlines the demise of essentially feminine values which challenged British colonialism in Ireland and sought to employ drama as 'a vehicle of propaganda' within that campaign. W.B. Yeats dismissed the inclusion of the ULT in his national theatre movement, and, in banishing the company back to Belfast, he ensured that the blinds were drawn on Enlightenment, on the potential of European ideology which might have informed that of Ulster theatre.

The movement's original and short-lived objectives transferred to a localised strategy of building a 'citadel'. The failed ideology of the ULT fostered a tradition of Ulster comedy within which sectarianism, partner of colonialism, became a seemingly harmless folk culture. Exiled from an island-wide Revivalism by its architect Yeats, the regional citadel which the ULT set about constructing represented a monument to civic culture and a fortress against outside influences, an altogether masculine construction that shielded Ulster against the ideology of the Enlightenment which the ULT initially sought to promote. Divorced from European and Irish Revivalist influences, the theatre capitulated to local populism and an easy representation of 'prod' and 'taig' as quaint opposing factions. The Tyrone nationalist-feminist playwright Alice Milligan may have been deemed unsuitable for the citadel. She was never invited in.

In 1960, Sam Thompson's *Over the Bridge* depicted a socialism which attempted to contest sectarianism. Thompson introduced a form of urban social realism which had appeared before in Ulster theatre – St John Ervine's *Mixed Marriage* (1911) is an example. (Notably, Ervine's play was not produced in the North until 1927, and opened at the Abbey Theatre in Dublin.) The production of *Over the Bridge* ensured that for Ulster theatre there was no retreat back over that bridge and cosier rural hearths are replaced by urban images of conflict and sectarianism.

For Charabanc Theatre Company, founded in 1983, the simple European axiom at that time of an equation of women's writing with feminism is unfounded in Northern Ireland. A sociological background to feminism and the Women's Movement in Northern Ireland forms an introduction to the central chapters. Devlin, Jones and Reid together create a community in which women's lives are foregrounded to document and appraise cultural history (Reid), to illustrate an alternative feminine process (Devlin), or to celebrate and liberate (Jones). While these three writers share a city and a gender, their imaginative domains thrive independently.

Devlin creates a trio of young women in *Ourselves Alone* and perhaps a more individually absorbing trio in *After Easter*. A closed republican patriarchy rules the lives of the young women in the first text, and that domination is exorcised by the character of Greta and, to an extent, her whole family in the second. Where there can be no freedom within the world of the freedom fighters in West Belfast, *After Easter* posits a psychic freedom, individual and hard won, a metaphor of a new Northern Ireland.

For Reid, the boundaries which may have been transgressed by the men of Ulster in two world wars have created a very real barrier for the women back home. Their lives are barricaded in by memories of lost lives. In *Tea in a China Cup* and *The King of the Castle*, matriarchs become surrogate males in a lonely society. While exits provide possible solutions, it is the outsider's or emigrant's eye that provides the analytical device for interrogation of a society which has suffered so much for so little apparent gain.

Jones, with Charabanc, has written the most subtle indictment of Northern Ireland society in *Somewhere Over the Balcony* and *The Girls in the Big Picture*. Both plays illustrate the efforts of the disenfranchised to become enfranchised. The 'colonised' of Divis Flats have become the 'colonisers', converting mayhem and social deprivation into a system of power and control. 'On a day like today, you could be anywhere' is the refrain and indeed, within the inversions, there is a comic truth in the statement. The voyages of discovery in *Hang All the Harpers*, *A Night in November* and *Women on the Verge of HRT* are matched by the smaller rebellions and revelations of *Stones in His Pockets*. In these texts, specific gender is secondary to cultural liberation, as men as often as women embark on these journeys.

For all three writers, the closed form of naturalism may accommodate the closed worlds which are represented (*Ourselves Alone*, *Tea in a China Cup*, *Weddins, Weeins and Wakes*). Jones is continually breaking the rules and spins other forms which deserve non-closure. She takes both an audience and her characters on unlikely journeys where the final destination is sometimes sunnier than expected. Devlin in *After Easter*, as the title suggests, seeks epiphanies and formal means within which to express them.

While exit routes vary from Reid's literal emigrations to Jones's comic inversions and Devlin's inner journeys, vehicles of form not provided by the ULT's legacy are much needed. Devlin's exposition of an offensive patriarchy in *Ourselves Alone* makes feminist statements but, within the socio-political context of West Belfast republicanism, can do no more than represent patriarchy and the plight of the women who endure its reign. In *After Easter*, she secures a new mode of representation where the diagnostic methodology of *Ourselves Alone*, like that of McGuinness in *The Factory Girls*, mutates towards the realisation of feminist form. *After Easter* is reminiscent of McGuinness's *Carthaginians* and provides a link with the final chapter, in which his work is inscribed as feminist.

The gender of writing produced is more important than the sex of the author and I analyse McGuinness's plays as feminist paradigms. His articulation of feminist theory provides a vocabulary of gender which relates back to the Irish Literary Revival, to Joyce and Beckett and their re-creations of identity as hybrid, encompassing male and female. *The Factory*

Girls, *Observe the Sons of Ulster Marching Towards the Somme*, *Carthaginians*, *Someone Who'll Watch Over Me* and *Mary and Lizzie* espouse and formulate a feminist ideal. McGuinness removes his characters into manufactured environments – a Beirut prison cell, a factory manager's office, a Derry graveyard, the fields of the Somme – which provide sites for subjunctive possibilities. His sense of form has often defied critics, who are more comfortable with fixed naturalism. At the end of *Carthaginians*, Dido defines the non-closure of the text: 'What happened? Everything happened, nothing happened, whatever you want to believe, I suppose.' There are no dictums, simply choices, 'whatever you want to believe'.

The playwrights in *The Girls in the Big Picture* have looked back at their times to map an unpalatable patriarchy which has been forged by both men and women in Northern Ireland. They have also envisioned futures. It is time to move on, to recover from 'the shock of gender', to imagine . . . [4]

1 Partition and absence
The Ulster Literary Theatre,
W.B. Yeats and Alice Milligan

The Victorian acceptance of the arts as refinement and reflection of culture was marked in Belfast by the opening of the newly built Grand Opera House in 1895, 'promoted from the first as the most respectable of establishments'. A decade later, the 'failed experiment' of the Grand Opera House as a venue for the 'risen classes' was manifest in its policy transformation. In 1904, the theatre's subtitle indicated its redirection: 'The most respectable of establishments' became 'The Palace of Varieties', a music hall 'for the masses.' Ophelia Byrne states that while Dublin and London were welcoming theatre 'back to respectable society', Belfast was judged as 'an icy place for theatre, a disastrous place to play, uniquely philistine, a purely industrial city'.[1]

In Dublin, W.B. Yeats, Lady Gregory and Edward Martyn had formed the Irish National Theatre Society. The founding ideology was based on a reinterpretation of the heroic past to inform a national future. Presentation of 'the deeper thoughts and emotions of Ireland' would 'show that Ireland is not the home of buffoonery and of easy sentiment, as it has been represented, but the home of an ancient idealism'.[2] Lady Gregory's mission statement does not mention nationalism, or political futures. In contrast, the Protestant National Association in the North was driven by political ideology and, particularly, nationalism. As Lady Gregory, Yeats and Martyn plotted an Irish Literary Revival, with theatre as the key promotional mechanism, a political revival was gathering force in Belfast, with the idea, too, of theatre as *its* propagandist mechanism.

Background to the Ulster Literary Theatre

At the turn of the twentieth century in the North of Ireland the political values of the preceding century, deriving from the United Irishmen of 1798, were still prevalent amongst Presbyterian liberals. The cause of national independence, of freedom from colonial power, was central to an enlightened minority. As Yeats, Lady Gregory and others gathered at her homes, Duras and Coole Park, another collective met at Loretto Cottage, home of Joseph Campbell, in North Belfast. Campbell, David Parkhill (Lewis Purcell) and Bulmer Hobson were leading members of the Protestant National Association, a mix of Irish nationalism and Protestant liberalism whose objective was the realisation of an independent Ireland. The perspective, definitions and visions of nationalism were not congruent: Yeats's nationalism was based on a revival of ancient heroism, the Northerners' on one nation ousting British rule. The contesting ideologies, based on differing priorities, never had the opportunity of proper discourse and debate, and from an early stage parted company.

Sam Hanna Bell's anecdotal account of Parkhill and Hobson's well-meaning approach to the members of the National Theatre Society in 1902 denies its consequences, and uncritically celebrates a dubious achievement. Bell quotes a letter he received from Hobson: 'Annoyed by Yeats, we decided to write our own plays – and we did.'[3] That decision, informed by personal and, perhaps, political irritation, has shaped the history and tenor of theatre in Ulster.

The narrative history of the Ulster Literary Theatre, as the pioneers named themselves in 1904, is well documented by Bell, by playwright and actor Rutherford Mayne, by critic Margaret McHenry, and by actor Whitford Kane.[4] Bell recounts that the ULT founders sought political nationalism within the framework of 'Liberty, Equality, Fraternity', and cultural fusion through the ideology of the Literary Revival in the South of Ireland. They nominated a title – The Ulster Branch of the Irish Literary Theatre – and in November 1902 produced Yeats's *Cathleen Ni Houlihan* and *The Racing Lug* by James Cousins. The productions were assisted by actors Dudley Digges and Maire Quinn from the Dublin company, and it was Maud Gonne who granted the rights for *Cathleen*, claiming that the play had been written for her. Yeats, however, had not agreed to the rights and in 1904, when the 'Ulster Branch' wished to produce *Cathleen* again, the National Theatre Company not only demanded royalties, but, as Bell recounts, informed the Northern company that it had no authority to state that it was a branch of their national company. Bell bluntly summarises the response: 'They re-named their company the ULT and applied themselves to the task of writing their own plays.'[5]

Alongside the Northern theatre venture, the literary review *Uladh* was established in November 1904 to promote 'the product of the Ulster genius'. The first editorial defines Ulster's separatism, which would be expressed in forms 'more satiric than poetic'. It also announced that 'Ulster has its own way of things'.[6] In February 1905 the next edition had defined 'the way of things', stating:

> We have not striven to erect a barrier between Ulster and the
> rest of Ireland; but we aim at building a citadel in Ulster for
> Irish thought and art achievements such as exists in Dublin. If
> the result is provincial rather than national, it will not be our
> fault, but due to local influences over which we have no
> control.[7]

A mission statement that employs negatives and abdicates responsibility for the outcome is odd indeed. The irreparable split between North and South was enshrined within the columns of *Uladh* and the forging of a regional identity within a manufactured 'citadel' had begun.

For most of the playwrights of the ULT, sectarianism became the central theme. In Belfast the focus on local issues separated the ULT from the theatre movement in the South. Bell's account of the sequence of events clearly points to Dublin keeping Ulster out and lends credence to Edna Longley's broader political statement quoting Liam de Paor, who asks 'whether partition arose not merely from the refusal of Ulster Unionists to come under a Dublin Parliament, but also from a powerful but largely unconscious drive by Nationalists (in the South) to exclude Protestants'.[8] The ensuing cultural apartheid can be seen as a precursor of political partition, with the consequences contributing to theatre in Ulster today.

David Kennedy refers to the 'high political winds' blowing between the National Literary Theatre and its Ulster counterpart, but there were other 'political winds' blowing across Ulster at the time.[9] Exiled from the ideals of the Irish Revival, both culturally and politically, the ULT was denied the realisation of an essentially radical and feminine ideal, radical in its objective of ousting colonial power, feminine in its replacement not by a hegemony based on power but on empowerment. Culturally thrown back on their native Ulster resources, the movement had to forge a realistic identity within a dominant socio/political context that was at odds with the inherent pre-partition nationalism of its founding ideology. The consequences of a conscious Ulsterisation within theatre can be seen at an early stage in the ULT's development.

Myth as Ideological Framework

The reliance on myth as the cornerstone of the Irish National Theatre movement was based on Yeats's conviction that endorsing the heroism of the past could re-create the same values in the present. The recognition of myth as feminine is seen by Bell as an emasculation which is unwelcomed by the Ulster psyche. His tone of patronising charm, double-edged, returns us to the province of Ulster: 'notwithstanding the beauty of these tales, the heroes are too vast, too amorphous; they lack the savage salt of human vulgarity'.[10] 'The great virtues, the great joys, the great privations come in the myths,' said Yeats, 'and, as it were, take mankind between their naked arms, and without putting off their divinity.' Bell interjects: 'There is nothing, I should say, more distasteful to an Ulsterman, of whatever persuasion, than to be hugged by a myth, unless, of course, he has had the privilege of creating it.'[11] Myth is 'feminine' and antithetical to the Ulster psyche. Within the work of the ULT, myth's local deployment became more a signifier of sectarianism and separatism. The provincialism and narrowness to which the movement quickly reverted were a reflection and endorsement of masculine values.

The choice of *Cathleen Ni Houlihan* as the play to mark the launch of the Ulster Theatre in 1902, and AE's (George Russell's) *Deirdre* in 1904, indicates the ULT's awareness of myth as potential propaganda mechanism, and, at the same time, as a vehicle for the transcendence of prejudice and the masculinity of sectarianism. As Bell admits, given the political climate at that time, these plays were hardly likely to, and did not, elicit a broad popular response.

Gerald MacNamara was a leading founding member of the ULT. His plays are among its best known and most revived today.[12] His disillusionment with community indifference to the company's aspirations did not immediately affect its predilection for the mythological framework. Hobson's *Brian of Banba* (1904) and Campbell's *Little Cowherd of Slainge* (1905) were reviewed as 'poetic dramas recalling the heroic past in the style of Yeats' and ran alongside plays which were grounded in local themes – Lewis Purcell's *The Enthusiast* (1905), Rutherford Mayne's *The Turn of the Road* (1906) and Purcell's *The Reformers* (1904). But it is in MacNamara's *Thompson in Tir na nÓg* (1912) that a symbiosis of the ancient heroic and the not-so-heroic present attempts to use the former to satirise the latter. In this historic combining of two mythologies, the 'green' and the 'orange', MacNamara set the stage for the future, while his play was threatened by assault from the rivets of the shipyard workers.

In MacNamara's text, Orangeman Andy Thompson has been 'blew up' by his own gun at the mock Battle of Scarva, an annual re-enactment of the Battle of the Boyne, to be transported to Tir na nÓg, where Grania is despatched by the king to woo Andy and hence discover his cultural background. The constant juxtaposition of archaic (Grania) and colloquial (Thompson) dialogue with the stunted presence of Andy in suit, bowler hat and Orange sash presents an ingenious collage of comic inversion and opposition:

> THOMPSON: Sure I told you I was on King William's side. Of
> course we won the day.
> GRANIA: Why do you say 'of course'? The fortunes of war are
> so uncertain.
> THOMPSON: Sure it wasn't a real fight. It was a sham fight.
> GRANIA: But have you been in a real fight?
> THOMPSON: O aye, I was in a scrap in Portadown last Sunday.
> GRANIA: And whom were you fighting in Portadown?
> THOMPSON: The Hibernians.
> GRANIA: The Hibernians! But are not all the people in Eirinn
> Hibernians?
> THOMPSON: Talk sense, woman dear.
> GRANIA: Many changes must have come over Eirinn since the
> days of Cuchulain and Oisin. Then we were all Hibernians. I
> wish, dearest Thompson, that you were a Hibernian too.
> THOMPSON: You'll never see the day. And what's more, I'll
> have nothing more to do with you, for I'm no believer in
> mixed marriages.[13]

Grania's world here is counterpointed by Thompson's closed prejudice, which presents itself as rational and logical, a masculine propensity. Like Swift's Gulliver, Thompson's unquestioned certainties are signifiers of a closed and unimaginative ontology. Finally, Andy has to choose between learning Gaelic, assimilation into the tribe, or death at the stake.

Thompson in Tir na nÓg was allegedly commissioned by the Gaelic League and turned down on the grounds that it 'travestied Celtic mythology'.[14] The play seems to have backfired in both directions, a classic case of intentionality versus reception. Produced in Belfast in 1912, in its care not to alienate the audience it attempted to convert – 'its subtlety escaped the offender whom it was endeavouring to chastise'.[15] Ironically, it became one of Ulster's most popular plays, the champion of the Orange Order, for which the play confirmed its worst fears of the intractability and blood thirst of Irish nationalism.[16] The play also instated sectarianism as a popular subject for comic treatment.

MacNamara's sequel, *Thompson on Terra Firma* (1934), as the title suggests, implants the Gaelic-speaking Thompson back among his Orange family. Like Gulliver ascending the stairs of the family home backwards on all fours as a Houyhnhnm, Thompson is a deranged embarrassment. The accident which sent him to Tir na nÓg is repeated to bring him back 'to his senses' and the 'real' world. The values of this 'real' Orange world are reinstated. *Thompson on Terra Firma* can be seen as a metaphor for the failed ideals of the ULT. That metaphor includes a depiction of the device of myth within the play as the political appropriation of myth by nationalism. If, inadvertently, *Thompson in Tir na nÓg* portrayed myth as the embodiment of not only nationalism but sacrificial death for its cause, the identification of myth with the 1916 Easter Rising bound it 'inextricably and fixedly to a theocentric vision which was Catholic, Republican and, to the Protestant north, heretical'.[17] The function of myth was thus identified with nationalism, and seen as the preserve of the nationalist South of Ireland, by the unionist North.

The mythic elements of the feminine, timeless, prehistoric, unfixed, are replaced by the male, the temporal and the historic. This is the provenance where 'nothing' is 'more distasteful than to be hugged by a myth'. *Thompson in Tir na nÓg* marks the end of a cycle and the later play, *Thompson on Terra Firma*, in making no attempt to justify the possibilities of its predecessor, ineffably accepts and, indeed, promotes the values of a Protestant/Orange ethic which would have been unpalatable to the founders of the ULT two decades earlier.

Sexuality and Rejection of Modernism

The ULT might have embraced the values of later Revivalism – Modernism, as embodied by James Joyce and J.M. Synge – if they had not been 'snubbed' by the instigator, Yeats. From McNamara's 1909 text *The Mist that Does Be on the Bog* there is no evidence of an appreciation of the roots and implications of later Revivalism. The play parodies the language of Synge and his West of Ireland field trips:

> BRIDGET: Good evening kindly lady, it's welcome you are, but
> it's a wild and stormy day, God Bless us to be out in the
> mountain side with the white mists driving up like shrouds

> from the rocky shores of Lough Corrib.
>
> CISSIE: This is just the sort of place I have always pictured in my imagination.[18]

The play within the play, which Belfast Cissie and Gladys have retired to the West to rehearse, is aptly titled 'What's All the Stir About', referring to the riots on reception of *The Playboy of the Western World*. The dialogue is exaggerated stage Irish and literal facts are swathed in similar language:

> GLADYS: Do you think he will be comin' home by the long gap and the wind rising up from the North East and him burdened down by the weight of drink?[19]

The 'Ulster common sense' subtext of both extracts is audible. Cissie and Gladys, in their wholehearted adoption of the parodied culture, provide the comedy. They are portrayed as willing dupes, completely entranced by their newly discovered culture. The parody is based on Synge's *The Shadow of the Glen*, where the tramp's 'blather' is pitted against Nora's pragmatism and her disinterest in the climatic soul of the Wicklow Hills. She says in Synge's text:

> For what good is a bit of farm with cows on it, when you do be sitting looking out from a door and seeing nothing but the mists rolling down the bog and the mists rolling up the bog.[20]

MacNamara's *The Mist that Does Be on the Bog* is a comedy which depends for effect on parodied language and ridiculous situations. While the women are rehearsing, or in raptures about the ambience of the West of Ireland, cousin Fred practises golf swings in the background, interjecting Ulsterisms and behaving like a middle-class Thompson. His masculine reluctance to partici- pate in the women's charade symbolises a broader masculinity, that of Ulster itself, separate and sensible. All the characters, including the locals, inhabit a pastiche world of mist and bogs, turf and blather. The central nuance of Synge's work, sexuality, is entirely ignored in a simple comic rendering of its superficialities.

MacNamara's parody does not touch on the issues that caused 'the stir' of the play within the play, Synge's perceived anti-nationalism in terms of sexual ethics. Synge's cosmopolitan sense of the sexual and its place is summed up by his own comment on the response to *The Shadow of the Glen:*

> On the French stage the sex element of life is given without the
> other balancing elements. I restored the sex element to its
> natural place, and the people were so surprised they saw sex
> only.[21]

In comparison to Nora (*The Shadow of the Glen*), Gladys and Cissie are positively asexual. Ulster removes 'sex' and, as D.E.S. Maxwell points out in reference to *Uladh* editorials, 'the theocratic Catholicism of the South had its Protestant counterpart' in the North.[22] While the ULT could attack other elements of Puritanism, the sexual seems to be taboo in its absence from the texts.

If the device of myth, central to the first phase of the Revival, could be absorbed and modified within the ULT genre, the inherent sexuality of the latter part of the Revival, of the Modernists, could not. By establishing myth as 'green' and plain Ulster vernacular as 'orange', and by pitting the two against each other, an easy comic form developed. Both traditions could laugh at each other, if not at themselves. Both could witness each other's stereotypes and the complex subject of sectarianism could be simplified within the comic form.

Sectarianism

Representations of sectarianism in Ulster and its characterisation through culture and ethnicity have pervaded the Ulster Theatre from its inception. As sectarianism has historically been constituted and reconstituted, so too has its representation in theatre. The religious label attached to sectarianism simplifies the complexities embodied within cultural and ethnic traditions. Desmond Bell's summary could be a commentary on the plays of Sam Thompson, and of Martin Lynch and John Boyd in the 1970s and 1980s:

> The two communities identify each other and themselves by
> reference to religious affiliation. And Loyalism in particular
> certainly utilises religious representations in its political
> discourse. However, in Northern Ireland religious

> identifications serve fundamentally as ethnic markers
> for communities with conflicting political aspirations.
> These aspirations are the product of a specific colonial
> situation.[23]

That matters of such difference, which governed life and perceptions of it in Northern Ireland, could be largely ignored by playwrights suggests a total abdication of the founding values of the ULT.

It was not until 1907, with MacNamara's *Suzanne and the Sovereigns*, that the ULT hit on its successful formula, a mixture of history and mythology within a contemporary setting. The play itself represents the first Ulster representation of staged sectarianism. Suzanne is a female version of the later Thompson. She falls hopelessly in love with Catholic King James II in loyalist Sandy Row and a local deputation is sent to Amsterdam to rally William III to the rescue. Rutherford Mayne states that the play 'might easily have had the same result as throwing a lit match into a barrel of gunpowder'. The production was quoted as 'a complete triumph', but was it?[24] The play effected the company's promotion to the large-scale venue of the Grand Opera House and, in retrospect, this move may have heralded the ULT's downfall. MacNamara's comic conversions of staunch Protestants to a Catholic orientation is matched in the early satires by individual transitions from an emphatically Protestant work ethic to artistic or even socialist endeavours – Purcell's *The Enthusiast* (1905), Mayne's *The Turn of the Road* (1906) and *The Drone* (1909). But the presentation of stereotypical caricatures refuted analysis and the ULT's original framework of reason and enlightened humanism was debased almost to the level of low comedy. The pattern created a genre in which sectarianism appeared, if not ethically acceptable, then harmless, almost quaint.

Both Kennedy and, later, the poet John Hewitt, see 'this skating over the thin ice of local prejudices'[25] as a form of artistic abdication. Certainly, the stereo-typed images of mythic queens, men in bowler hats and sashes and Catholic-loving philanthropists avoid any level of social or political analysis to almost legitimise sectarianism as a colourful local custom. The poet W.R. Rodgers, in a critical article on Ulster, can define sectarianism as an anthropologist's dream: 'it is this diversity and interplay of opposites that makes Ulster life such a rich and fascinating spectacle'.[26] The 'rich and fascinating spectacle' has some hideous manifestations.

An obvious exception to this analytical lack is St John Ervine's *Mixed Marriage* (1911). In this play sectarianism is represented as a product of political confusion and ignorance which manifests itself in domestic chauvinism. The role of woman is central and sectarianism is a function of male hegemony, whose treble articulation is political, religious and sexist. Factually based on the 1907 dockers' strike, when political and economic insecurity allowed hidden prejudices to float freely to the surface, the play is a maze of human confusion, contradiction and ignorance, embodied in the key character Rainey, patriarch, speech-maker and bigot. The mute power base, inhabited by the portrait of King Billy on the living-room wall, is shared by Rainey, whose public performances to the Orange Lodge are paralleled by a monosyllabic stubbornness at home. Public and private spheres are at loggerheads within Rainey's psyche and are consistently thrown into relief by his wife's astuteness. Mrs Rainey, as John Cronin has pointed out, is 'the Juno Boyle of the piece'[27] and, like Juno, endures and analyses male folly without doing anything about it. At the end of the play, when the mob is raging outside the door and Nora (anticipating a later classic victim, O'Casey's Bessie Burgess) is shot, Mrs Rainey's impotent complicity is framed within a single moment of intense gendered isolation:

> RAINEY: (*as if dreaming*) A wus right. I know A wus right.
> MRS RAINEY: (*weeping a little, and patting him gently*) Aw, my
>   poor man, my poor man.[28]

Mixed Marriage presents woman as the embodiment of an unfulfilled integrity whose power exists only in its ability to camouflage itself to maintain the empowerment of the male. Mrs Rainey's ability to encompass broad philosophies within the simplest language is pitted against the self-importance of the men and always with irony:

> MRS RAINEY: Can't ye see, they're doing the very thing ye
>   want Irelan' to do?
> MICHAEL: There'll be no salvation fur Irelan' til a man is born
>   that dussen care a God's curse fur weemen. They're hangin'

> about the neck o' the lan' draggin' her down.
>
> MRS RAINEY: (*aside*) Aw let the men talk. Sure it keps them quiet.[29]

While Mrs Rainey can dance around her less intelligent brethren, her acute awareness of their identity diminishes her own.

The political plexus is rich, complicated and highly contemporary in its pessimism. As Cronin says: 'It is a sad comment on the repellent sameness of Ulster sectarianism that the issues Ervine dealt with ... remain just as vivid and unresolved in the Belfast of the 1980s.'[30] The difficult question is why did the ULT ignore a play of such sophistication and contemporary relevance? The answer may be found in a comment by Kennedy on a later play by Ervine, *Boyd's Shop*: 'Presbyterian Ulster liked this picture of itself.'[31] The picture presented by *Mixed Marriage* is less palatable. Free from sentiment and nostalgia, the play presents a grim image of Orange insularity and an equally grim image of republicanism, both textured by overt sexism. Woman is imaged as highly rational, unprejudiced and oppressed. The play interrogates assumptions and a reality which is neither mythic nor historical and certainly not comic. A genre of realism within which prejudice is critically examined has been founded by a Northern playwright but ignored by the producers of the ULT.

Sam Thompson's *Over the Bridge* exposed a rigid and often subtle suppression of freedom which might express a challenge to unionist supremacy.[32] Paddy Devlin sums up the ethos:

> Thompson strove to uncover the mechanisms which manipulated education and the general social conduct of Protestant workers which determined their position within the general spectrum of society. He expressed his ideology consistently and forcefully, mostly through the minds and tongues of trade-unionists of a pronounced anti-loyalist and anti-establishment persuasion. His philosophy comes through as rational, straightforward, problem orientated.[33]

Thompson's interpretation of sectarianism is one of abstraction, an uncontrollable virus which strikes the collective rather than the individual –

signified by the offstage 'mob'. Thompson's imagery is of the impalpable presence, what Stewart Parker refers to as the 'seepage, a kind of fog of religiotics which seeps in everywhere':[34]

> RABBIE: They crawl round the boats and through the workshops fuming the flames of bigotry with their plausible double-meaning talk and it's the same wherever you go in this country ... nobody wants to know where the actions of a mob begins or where it ends for that matter.
> FOX: You can nail nothing on anybody without proof, Rabbie. That's the law.[35]

But, for all its Marxist diagnosis, linguistic fluidity and parabolae, *Over the Bridge* is, formally, masculine. The structure is highly conventional: situation–crisis–denouement. The play is closed. Within this arena, women are sharply focused mirror reflections of their male partners: Nellie is as greedy and self-satisfied as husband George; Martha's conversation is based on obsessive anecdotes of Rabbie's persecution for his socialist principles. As in later plays, and particularly in the work of Christina Reid, women perpetuate the ideologies of their men. Dramatically, Thompson uses woman to demonstrate the totality of the social 'seepage', as Parker says, 'through the workplace' but also through the domestic environs of the backstreet homes.

While the ULT endorsed cultural fusion within the nationalism of the Yeatsian Revival, its failure of nerve and its dependence on commercial rather than political development are demonstrated by its inability to confront the issues of later Revivalism, sexuality of both form and content, and the rejection of patriarchy. An appendage to this in the North is the absence of a single suffragist play despite the propagandist theatre of the Irish Women's Franchise League and Maud Gonne's Inghinidhe na hÉireann (Daughters of Ireland), who were responsible for progressing the early ULT productions.[36]

Female Absence

The contemporary work of Irish feminist historians and critics has done much to rectify the traditional patriarchal view of the role of women in the time of the Ulster and Irish Literary Theatres. That a woman's place was in the home, in service to the family, or outside that domain, as carer for the sick and poor, was the incontestable accepted norm.[37] The nationalist construct of woman was vigorously promoted as that of home-maker and spiritual counsellor to the young, the interchangeable motifs being that of hearth and altar. What, until recently, has not been fully acknowledged is the challenge by women in their thousands to this stereotype. 'While women were not expected to have any public presence at all',[38] and that has been the received image, in a host of necessarily separatist organisations they radically campaigned on issues as diverse as Home Rule or the Union, land reform and the franchise. The debarment of women from most public organisations necessitated the foundation of their own. The act of revisionism is succinctly defined by historian Margaret Ward, who states that, 'because women have been so marginal in the consciousness of those who have researched events, their significance remains hidden'.[39] Women's contribution to history and a changing culture during the early twentieth century has been critically revised and, as stated by Myrtle Hill and Vivienne Pollock, traditional images of passivity and patriarchal definition are 'replaced by a series of more complex images reflecting the actual tensions and contradictions of both individual and collective experience'.[40]

The establishment of numerous significant organisations by and for women in the late nineteenth and early twentieth centuries is testimony to the resourcefulness and political acumen of women who were denied access to any form of government outside the boundaries of domesticity. While privileged women had access to higher education, it was not until 1908 that women were accepted into the universities on an equal basis with men.[41]

Within the ULT there is little evidence of the presence or influence of women except as relatives of the main players. Occasional and one-off plays by Helen Waddell, Josephine Campbell and Patricia O'Connor were performed. Caricatures by Grace Plunkett feature smoke-filled rooms with no female presence except in stage depictions, where there is an occasional woman, almost a single physical adornment to the male performers.[42]

Margaret McHenry alludes to the dearth of women contributors as 'possibly' having been caused by 'the close association with politics maintained by the originators of the Ulster Literary Theatre'. She states:

'Not only are practically all the Ulster playwrights men, but they put most of their best drawn characters among the ranks of their own sex. They could not, however, make all of their plays totally without heroines.'[43] These are pertinent remarks by the only female chronicler of the ULT. Bell, Kennedy, Mayne and Hagel Mengel do not refer to gender issues within their studies. Given that McHenry conducted her research by interviewing key players within the movement, the lack of comment by them on female participation is further testimony to the status, or lack of it, of women within theatre at the time. Male commentators can hardly be accused of sexist revisionism if the role of women was as negligible as it would seem. However, the omission of the work of one Ulster poet and playwright from the annals of the ULT is glaring. Alice Milligan was a prodigious patriot and advocate of nationalism. She has been described as being in the 'forefront of the Nationalist and literary movement, recognised, respected and admired'.[44]

Milligan was born 1866 in Omagh, County Tyrone, and enjoyed a privileged upbringing, collaborating with her father on the compiling and publication of texts on matters of local interest. She had an equally privileged education, attending King's College London, where she became a member of the Irish Literary Society in 1893. Two years later, back in Belfast, she founded and edited the *Northern Patriot*, whose editorial stated the advancement of 'the good old cause that has braved unceasing persecution for seven centuries'.[45] While the reasons for Milligan's departure from the journal after only three issues are unclear, her fervent nationalism and adherence to the tropes of the Celtic Revival – the restoration through literature of an ancient self-esteem to a new Irish nation – found voice in the establishment of another periodical, the *Shan Van Vocht*. Milligan edited this journal until 1899 and its title and manifesto from the anonymous poem celebrating the 1798 rebellion represent the manifesto of the Protestant National Association, the founders of the ULT:

> Yes! Ireland shall be free
> From the centre to the sea;
> Then hurrah for liberty
> Says the Shan Van Vocht.[46]

Throughout this period and in the first decade of the new century, Milligan moved within the circles of the élite of the Revivalist movement. Yeats, Maud Gonne, Standish O'Grady, Roger Casement and James Connolly were associates.[47] For Bulmer Hobson she was a mentor and role model as a political and literary figure. Of her collection of poetry, *Hero Lays*, published in 1908, he states: 'they are unlike anything we have seen in Ireland. They strike a new note in our literature.'[48] Other contemporary commentaries on Milligan's literary status, if tainted by patriotic predilection, testify to the cultural esteem in which she was held. Maud Gonne's autobiography notes a meeting with Milligan in Belfast: 'I thought,' she states, 'Dublin would have to look to its laurels if it were not to be outdone in literary journalism by Belfast.'[49] But it is Thomas MacDonagh's eulogy that is best known. In an article on living Irish poets for the *Irish Review* in 1914, he writes:

> I should like to begin with the best . . . I have no difficulty of
> choice . . . It is meet that this Irish national poet should be a
> woman. It is meet that she, like so many of the leaders of the
> Irish Volunteers, should be of Northeast Ulster. Alice Milligan,
> Ulster Protestant, Gaelic Leaguer, Fenian, friend of all Ireland,
> lover of Gaelic Catholic as of her own kith . . . is the most Irish
> of living poets, and therefore the best.[50]

Such high-profile praise is testimony to Milligan's position as a poet of the nationalist literary movement. Her plays demonstrate a feminism that was subordinate only to the nationalist cause.

The complexities of the alliance between feminism and nationalism in Ireland have been well documented.[51] While Terry Eagleton equates male/female opposition with that of colonial oppressor and oppressed and the universal 'right of a group victimised . . . to be on equal terms with others',[52] the central dilemma for Irish suffragists was that they were campaigning for a vote to a parliament from which they were seeking independence. Declan Kiberd sees the linkage of Irish suffragism with 'West Britonism' as verging on the 'pathological'.[53] But this was exactly the essence of the feminist/nationalist dilemma, where women were criticised 'for putting the interests of their sex before that of the Nation'. Ward cites this and the claim by Maud Gonne's Inghinidhe na hÉireann that to accept enfranchisement by a hostile parliament would be 'humiliating'.[54] Milligan's close involvement with the

Inghinidhe and with Gonne's ideology ensured that she shared the 'patho-logical' ideology. Her feminism and particular brand of nationalism are de-monstrated in the opposition to a Yeatsian 'Celtic Twilight' dialectic.

Milligan wrote to *United Ireland* following a visit by Yeats to her home in Belfast in 1893. She registered concern about a literary movement that was removed from the reality of struggle: 'Irish literature cannot be developed in any hedged-in peaceful place, whilst a conflict is raging around. It must be in the thick of the fight.' Yeats's response in the following issue is as subliminal as it is patronising and evidences a misogyny that is shrouded in symbol and refers to a 'beauty' which belies the tone and facts of Milligan's correspond-ence. He writes: 'She ... wrote you a very beautiful letter ... It is ... a pleasure to be misunderstood when the misunderstanding helps to draw out such a beautiful letter.'[55] This arrogance is matched some years later when Yeats requests Milligan to postpone the 1798 centenary celebrations in Belfast, so that he may more easily promote his first season of plays for the Irish Literary Theatre.[56]

Propagandist and idealist again clashed when Yeats tried to appropriate credit for work which he had not witnessed and which had been promoted by Milligan on behalf of the Gaelic League. Milligan replied to Yeats's 'admiration' that a play in the Irish language had solicited enthusiastic responses by chastising him for referring to work which he had not seen and in which she 'had taken part'. She further categorised Yeats as a 'West Briton', managed to mention the success of her 1798 celebrations and finally reclaimed nationalist theatre experiments as the initial property of the Gaelic League rather than the Irish Literary Theatre.[57] This is a strong and clever rejoinder, one which could not be patronised with adjectives relating to 'beauty'.

These encounters are cited to highlight Milligan's resistance to male appro-priation of female intentionality, a process which is further demonstrated by Milligan's texts and the essentially male response to them. Furthermore, these public debates reflect the mixed ideology of the Revival.

Milligan's *The Last Feast of the Fianna, A Dramatic Legend*, part one of an Ossianic trilogy, was chosen by Yeats to open the second season of the Irish Literary Theatre at the Gaiety Theatre, alongside Edward Martyn's *Maeve*. Milligan's play begins with all the adornments of feasting, contrasting with a deeply elegiac mood following the routing of the Fianna at Gabhra. Fionn's first utterance discards the inadequacies of Grania's female powers of enchantment in favour of Oisin's music, the single action that will lift hearts and the feast itself. Oisin's *caoin* for the death of his son Oscar has been, he declares, the last of his music-making. Grania chastises him for constantly mourning death and 'taking no heed to please the living'. Niamhe appears offering immortality in the land of eternal youth. Oisin is Niamhe's third choice – in fact he offers himself and in so doing denies his vow to the Fianna, an abdication which is treasonous.

Milligan accentuates this portrayal of the bard and warrior as dreamer and irresponsible escapist. He is 'not wise in the ways of women', and, as a 'dreaming poet', he 'has not learned three things are not to be looked for – leaves in winter, snow in summer, and silence in a woman'.[58] The analogy of dreaming poet and Yeatsian spiritualist is clearly and consistently emphasised within the text. Part two, *Oisin in Tir na nÓg*, does not attempt to portray a transformed Oisin. He is as aggressively bored by the joys of everlasting youth as he had been depressed in the real world of part one. To the piping of the fairy women, he retorts:

> Silence the music there
> Lest I slay you.

Of course, the irony of such an intention in the land of 'eternal youth' is obvious. Oisin's infatuation with Niamhe's beauty can terminate as suddenly and easily as it began. He falls victim to the same forces of 'enchantment' as those which drew him to Tir na nÓg in the first place. With less ceremony and an even more brutal abdication, this time of Niamhe, he rushes back to Ireland to find his Fianna.

Readings of the texts, and particularly Yeats's failure to grasp Milligan's sophisticated irony and veiled parody of male heroism, point to a critical obtuseness that cannot accommodate feminist ideology or the irony within which it is couched. While one critic mistakenly credits Milligan for 'producing the first completely Celtic Twilight play',[59] another diminishes the text with the feminine adjectives 'graceful' and 'slender' and on another occasion refers to it as 'consciously or even self-consciously poetic and mystical'.[60] The *Freeman's Journal* disparagingly refers to 'Miss Milligan's little drama' as 'simply a paraphrase from the old Gaelic story of Diarmuid and Grania'. The *Daily Express* refers to the 'charm' of the piece and states that 'If it has no other merits, it reproduces, at all events, in a vivid manner the main characteristics of the heroic age in Ireland.' Yeats's esoteric and subjective interpretation echoes those of the press: 'Miss Milligan's little play delighted me,' he says, 'because it has made in a very simple way, and through the vehicle of Gaelic persons, that contrast between immortal beauty and the ignominy and mortality of life which is the central theme of ancient art.' If this was, indeed, the central theme of ancient art, it was certainly not Milligan's contemporary interpretation of it. To make matters worse, Yeats requested that Milligan write an article to outline the mythical background to *The Last Feast of the Fianna*. Milligan's succinct reply requires no explanation: 'an audience of Kerry peasants would have no need of background information'.[61]

Milligan's biographer, Sheila Turner Johnston, relates that it was in the enthusiasm following the first visit by Yeats to Milligan in 1893 that she turned to drama by reworking a novel, *The Daughter of Donagh*. This was submitted to Lady Gregory, who rejected the text on behalf of the Irish Literary Theatre by stating that 'Yeats considered that it changed scene too often to be a practical proposition'.[62] Perhaps it was more than the scene changes that disturbed Yeats.

The Daughter of Donagh is an allegory of Cromwellian rule. It challenges colonialism and advocates the de-anglicisation of Ireland as the single prerequisite to a return to justice and equity. The narrative is linear and based on the exploits of the heroine, Onora. Her father has been evicted from his land and she witnesses his hanging. Her only solace is revenge, which she executes by marrying the soldier who has been granted the rights to her father's land.

The representation of Ireland is not that of heroic legend but of an enslaved community whose only hope of freedom lies with bandits who inhabit mountain caves. While the women haggle over food and a man to provide it, the priest describes the landscape as 'the wilds of Ireland'. There is nothing edifying in Milligan's evocation of past heroism, current colonialism, or the environments in which each has occurred. The play is a harrowing rendering of wrongdoing and of a war without possibilities.

Opposition to gender stereotyping is underlined, while the archetypal stereotype of the female goddess as subject is subverted and transformed. Onora is active subject, a real and living entity participating within the male culture of the fight for freedom, a stance which, as regarded by Maurice, 'for a woman would be "impossible"'. Milligan's feminism interrogates the authorised female figure, the conventional representation of woman. Militant feminism is refuted without endorsing the nationalism from which it emanated. Milligan re-creates Yeats in the character of Maurice, the West Briton who offers his hand in marriage and is rejected by Onora, whose vision is based on vengeance rather than love. Milligan's portrayal of conventional sexism in Maurice's misunderstanding of Onora also recalls the relationship between Yeats and Maud Gonne. Onora rejects Maurice and favours the indigenous warrior Seaghan. Besotted, Maurice stampedes on, ludicrously wooing a 'poor little hand, little white hand, trembling like a wounded bird'.[63] Yeats would hardly have appreciated the hyperbole.

Conclusion

So, quietly ignored by the Irish Literary Theatre, Milligan was not commissioned or produced by the ULT. Yet this exclusion may have been voluntary. Her poem 'Fionnuala', which she contributed to the second issue of *Uladh,* appeared alongside the very editorial that signalled the early dissolution of the ULT's original mission by introducing the 'provincial' in opposition to the 'national'. Milligan's nationalism would have abhorred even a hint towards a provincialism that dissociated itself from the rest of Ireland. So, too, Hobson's allegiance to theatre was short-lived. Historian Jonathan Bardon cites Hobson's involvement, as early as 1905, in founding a branch of the militantly separatist Irish Republican Brotherhood.[64] Radical politics of this potency could not find comfort within the Northern theatre movement. And Milligan's feminism, conveniently obscure for Southern critics, would have been scorned by the men of the Ulster movement, if they would have been capable of recognising it at all.

The loss to the literary legacy is significant in terms of the potential formative effect of a body of female work. Historically and culturally, easy stereotypes are challenged and transformed in Milligan's exceptionally modern analyses. As her biographer comments in congruence with feminist historians, 'the received view of history is the male view'[65] and within a context of historical revisionism 'there is little knowledge of the importance of Alice Milligan in a critical period in Irish history'.[66] A suitable appendage to this statement might be that neither is there any recognition of Alice Milligan as propagandist playwright, the very being which the ULT was founded to promote. In the words of Forrest Reid, writing in 1922 of the achievement of the ULT, there 'are only two forms of drama it has as yet mastered – folk comedy and fantastic farce'.[67] That brief and perhaps not entirely fair synopsis might have been enlivened by the inclusion of a playwright of Milligan's imaginative ability and feminist range.

The social and literary revolution as envisaged by Joyce and Synge did not enter the vocabulary of the ULT. The centrality of the feminine form and, in turn, of female sexuality, as characterised by Molly Bloom (*Ulysses*) and Nora (*The Shadow of the Glen*), and of anti-patriarchy, in the re-creation of identity (*The Playboy of the Western World*), is absent from MacNamara's *The Mist that Does Be on the Bog*. While this play parodies Synge's mannerism, MacNamara's anthropological exploits are presented as feminine whims of fancy. Male rationality is underlined through the character of Fred, who symbolises a broader masculinity, that of Ulster itself. *Irish* manhood, on the other hand, is epitomised by drunken blather and late-night journeys home across the bog, depicting a backward, unindustrialised, irresponsible nation.

Finally, in the treatment of sectarianism and the failure to attempt its analysis or accept its outcomes, the ULT created a tradition of satirical farce which kept theatre safely confined to rural quaintness, unchallenging images of Ulster, an Ulster that liked to see itself as friendly and benign in its cultures of division. In the words of John Hewitt, they 'had to shed precisely those elements which lie deep in the life of our people ∴ ... Religion and Politics. Not one syllable has emerged to betray the wee red lamp, or alternatively, the picture of King William on the wall, the concocting of fairy-tales in a local accent.'[68] It was not until the early 1960s, in the work of Sam Thompson, that the reality of sectarianism was presented to challenge unionist hegemony. The exception is Ervine's *Mixed Marriage*, which defines sectarianism by imaging domestic and public chauvinism and introduces woman as potential subject. The absence of this text from the ULT's programme until

1927 is further indication of the gradual abdication of their initial ideology.

The political framework, based on a concept of absolute power, a totally male prerogative, which goes some way towards defining Northern Irish ethnicity, is eventually supported by the drama of the ULT, a far cry from the founding manifesto. This legacy has been both endorsed and challenged by its inheritors, who have had to seek their own methods of dealing with it.

Yet, the ULT must be credited with having established the first regional theatre in Ireland. The company's theatrical, if not political, ambition was prodigious. Seasons at the Abbey Theatre in Dublin (1907–9), were followed by an English tour in 1911 and a tour of the United States in 1912. While residencies at the Grand Opera House continued until 1934, the name change to the Ulster Theatre in 1915 seems significant. Ophelia Byrne summarises comments by Forrest Reid and Sam Hanna Bell, all of which suggest a split in loyalties.[69] The ULT's achievement in founding and promoting an Ulster theatre genre and movement provided a dubious legacy to future generations. It is one whose language, ideology and form has been so firmly instated with sectarianism at its centre, that it took almost a century to move beyond its confines to contemplate a contemporary Modernism in Ulster within the work of Frank McGuinness, Marie Jones, Anne Devlin and Christina Reid. Sexual hybridity and identity, the man woman and the woman man, a feature of the Modernists, Joyce and Beckett in particular, have no space within early Ulster drama. Uncomplicated masculine values of binary opposites present a rational and ordered world. This supposed masculine rationale and order is interrogated by the women practitioners of the 1980s and 1990s.

2 An offensive patriarchy
Background to women in Northern Ireland

If the traditional female habitus has been seen as more private than public, domestic rather than social, and individual as opposed to collective, then its product will inevitably seem foreign to a masculine-led means of production. In 1991, in Belfast, the three main houses, the Grand Opera House, the Belfast Civic Arts Theatre and the Lyric Players Theatre, were controlled by male boards of directors. Since then, change has been essential and forced by conditions of funding and the legal requirements of equal opportunities policy. None the less, a flourish of women playwrights seems a far-off ideal. In this context, the commercial successes of Marie Jones are gratefully received exceptions for local audiences, of which the larger percentage is women.

In a critique of the situation in the Irish Republic, Victoria White states that 'the fashioning of national identity' has been male made. She suggests that an updating of that identity should include 'feminism and economics. If this happens,' she concludes, 'the women playwrights will follow.'[1] In Northern Ireland, the possibility of 'feminism' creating an identity is remote from the current political agenda. The Agreement reached by Northern politicians and the British and Irish governments in 1998 includes a clause on the promotion of women within politics and the public sector, an acknowledgement of the fact that there may indeed be a problem of representation.[2] The clause was eventually included following hard-fought negotiation by the Northern Ireland Women's Coalition (NIWC).

The following three chapters contextualise the work of three women writers, Marie Jones, Anne Devlin and Christina Reid, and the work of Charabanc Theatre Company within the social and political framework of Northern Ireland. The nexus of work and the conditions in which it has been achieved are inseparable. The social and political context is central to the playwrights, whether that context is endorsed or challenged by them. It is also central to an understanding of their texts.

Background to Feminism and the Women's Movement in Northern Ireland

The cultural constructs that have impeded a development of feminist perspectives in Northern Ireland are those relating to both the Irish Republic's constitution for nationalists and fundamentalist Christianity for the unionist community. The former's dictate of the place of women in the home is replicated by the latter's espousal of loyalty to the men of Ulster. The challenge to the relegation of women as literal and cultural servants is a challenge to the hegemony of church and state and, more importantly in Northern Ireland, to deeply held senses of history and tradition on both sides of a religious divide.[3]

Within this panorama of patriarchy, the central dilemma between party politics and feminist issues has plagued the history of feminism in twentieth-century Ireland. The nationalist/suffragist dichotomy has been discussed in Chapter 1, focusing on Alice Milligan, whose nationalism preceded her feminism in the mistaken assumption that liberation from colonialism equated with liberation from patriarchy. Decades later the same issues apply, and women have been victimised for transgressing boundaries of ideological, religious and political difference.

In the North women's crossings of party political and sectarian divides have been systematically and effectively quashed by opposing political hierarchies. Single-issue campaigns that have united women have been short-lived and sporadic, undermined by sectarianism from within local communities, as Lynda Walker (formerly Edgerton) illustrates.[4] These community campaigns are best exemplified by the demise of the movement of the Peace Women, whose high public profile could not sustain its cross-community dynamic.[5] The Peace Movement was formed in 1976 as the Women's Peace Movement, when three children, including a baby, were killed by a wounded gunman's getaway car. The driver had been shot by the British Army. The female leadership was pilloried by offensive and overt sexism, as well as a thinly disguised sectarianism, which masqueraded as political acumen. 'The explosion of female rage', as Bernadette Devlin[6] described the initiation of the movement, was unable to defend itself against the armoury of centuries' sectarian-based ideology.

In Northern Ireland it was not a lack of feminist consciousness but a fear of voicing that hidden consciousness that has ensured the slow progress of gender equality in the twentieth century (the Mrs Rainey syndrome of *Mixed Marriage*). The traditional role of women has been perceived as mothers and carers, as unseen supporters of fathers and husbands, keepers of hearth and altar.

The Northern Ireland Women's Rights Movement was born out of a 'desperation',[7] one which recognised the constraints of political and cultural traditions on the lives of women. The movement also recognised that within the sectarianism and poverty of Northern Ireland, the rights of women may have been perceived as 'a luxury'.[8] Twenty years later, the formation of the NIWC in 1996 responded to a similar desperation, and illustrates by its existence and support that the post-feminism of modern Europe has not reached Northern Ireland's shores.

The public lack of feminist awareness also relates to women's involvement in political practice at a grass-roots level, rarely achieving the prominence of mainstream governance, operating, as Lynda Edgerton states, 'under ground rather than over ground'.[9] Such tactics, she suggests, may even undermine the development of an equality agenda by reinforcing gender stereotyping. Women have organised and campaigned not only for their own interests but consistently for those of the general community, and usually at the margins rather than in the mainstream of political and social life. Images of women and children mounting local community protests in support of the Drumcree stand-off highlight the literal relegation to their own doorstep and, until recently, their lack of representation within the Orange Order. (The first protests by Orangemen at Drumcree parish church, County Armagh, occurred in 1995 when a traditional parade on the Sunday before the Twelfth of July, through the nationalist Garvaghy Road in Portadown, was blocked by the Royal Ulster Constabulary. Violence and civil unrest have been an annual occurrence at Drumcree and in other parts of Northern Ireland since that time.) Role conditioning is clearly stated in the faithful loyalty to husbands and sons, mirroring the supportive role of women in the opposite republican camp.[10] Women's attempts to lobby on issues that affect their everyday lives have been branded by their respective paramilitaries as 'Republican challenges to the state' (loyalist) or as 'collusion with opposing forces' (republican).[11] The very act of cross-community single-gender initiative threatens the patriarchal stronghold.

The formation of the NIWC, to introduce the voice of women to the official politics of Northern Ireland, was an expression of frustration and deeply felt ignominy by some who were exhausted by male perceptions and priorities, whether locally or from Westminster.[12] The language of negativity spelled stasis for a society that was already locked in competing ideologies, none of which were acknowledging or addressing women, all in a gender-specific framework of male hegemony. Also in recognition that since its founding in 1921 Northern Ireland had seen only three women elected as Members of Parliament, a campaigning organisation was formed.[13] The resulting electoral victories were testimony to changing forces engi-neered particularly by women who registered support for the inclusion of a feminine voice in the governance of Northern Ireland. Strongest support for the NIWC was won in North Down and South Belfast, wealthier constitu-encies that boast a larger percentage of educated professional women. Monica McWilliams (South Belfast) and Jane Morrice (North Down) were elected to the Northern Ireland Assembly in June 1998.

Within the language and mode of masculine politics in Northern Ireland, it is not surprising that when the NIWC insisted that the Agreement affirmed 'the right of women to full and equal participation', they were initially told that gender issues were not relevant. Eventually, a clause relating to the 'advancement of women in political life' was included in the final text of the Agreement. The deeply entrenched sexism of Northern politics is safely hidden beneath years of communal conflict, and challenged most significantly by women. It is an especially difficult challenge when the rest of the world has moved on and local male politicians can parade the usual argument that 'women are treated exactly like men', and, worse, the assertion that in Northern Ireland we inhabit a post-feminist society.

In Northern Ireland injustices have been highlighted and campaigned against by women largely acting as supporters of the rights of the men in their family circle. Injustice against women has rarely been voiced, even by women themselves. The facts of the consciousness of women in the North are well summarised by Suzanne Buckley and Pamela Lonergan:

> Participation in political awareness for Irish catholic women
> in the North has not led to a feminist consciousness. If any
> change occurs, it may stem from the stresses upon the
> traditional family . . . [which] could cause women to realise the
> nature of a patriarchal society. Such a realisation might cause
> them to question their relationship to present political
> activities.[14]

Perhaps the following anecdote, quoted by Edgerton, prefigures the work of women playwrights and particularly that of Anne Devlin in *Ourselves Alone*. The involvement of Edgerton's female in the civil rights movement is emphasised. Her past activism has led to a disillusioned and remote existence, far removed from the ideology for which she campaigned:

> On our night out, he goes off to the club. I put the children to
> bed. I arrange for the babysitter to come and then I get ready
> to go out. I go to the club, sit down and Peter, when he sees me,
> comes and buys me a drink. Then he goes off to talk to his
> friends. I sit all night on my own, and mostly buy my own

> drink. Then I go home. Peter has to stay, to help clear up the
> club. I then pay the babysitter and that's our night out.[15]

The final commentary from the former female civil rights activist is:

> He sits up there in the club talking about when he was in Long
> Kesh . . . This house is like Long Kesh to me. At least, he had
> friends to talk to inside. I'm here on my own staring at these
> four walls.[16]

Edgerton's anecdote describes a loneliness that is the living fear of Anne Devlin's female characters and a position to which, ironically, they propel themselves. The helplessness that pervades their male-dominated lives is a construct of cultural and political socialisation, dependent on traditions of love, motherhood and family. These values provide power and domestic amnesty to men.

The essence of this status quo is deeply ingrained in Ulster theatre, where the portrayal of women as domestic minders rarely encroaches upon their psychologies, or even describes them in terms of lives lived and characters shaped. With the exception of Frank McGuinness, the female psyche has seldom been portrayed by male playwrights beyond a stereotypical version of behaviour that depicts woman as the minder of hearth and obedient servant to male oligarchy.

3 Charabanc Theatre Company and Marie Jones
Not that kind of war

Interview with Marie Jones, May 2002

The Charabanc years have been well documented, as well as your own background at Orangefield Secondary School, where you were relegated to the drama class for bad behaviour! You then went on to work with James Young and became known as a comedy actress. So we start at the point where you were working collaboratively with Charabanc. Without that, could you envisage yourself having become a writer, through the ordinary channels that were available at that time in the 1980s in Northern Ireland? What Charabanc was doing was very different from the conventional models of theatre production.

I very much doubt that I would have written, but maybe I would have woken up one morning and thought that I wanted to write. Then I didn't recognise myself as a writer – I was just somebody who wanted to act and I wanted to do plays that were relevant to me and the people around me, and so, in retrospect, it was a way of finding a voice and getting a place to start from. It was years before I would even call myself a writer. Even though I was penning all the material and I loved doing it, it was very much a function in order to allow me and the company to perform material which was real and important to us as actresses in Northern Ireland at that time.

So what was your first solo work, or was there such a thing?

It's very hard to pinpoint. The process was slow and ongoing. With all the collaboration, I did have to go off alone with the characters and have a certain amount of freedom to move them about, to develop them in my head. At the same time, I didn't want to become a slot machine – write this, write that. I had to have a sense of freedom, to be able to move those characters, to change them. Although we talked a lot about the characters, actually making them real, making their words real was very solo because that's something you can only do alone, you can't do that collaboratively. You can do the rest, you can do the story, you can decide where the play is going, what we want to say, but even then there was some licence to go down certain roads that we had not talked about; but you can only do that when you sit alone with the characters.

Charabanc was very much about presenting the lives of women and in all the company's interviews feminism was out, beyond the pale, and yet I see you as not only presenting women's lives but promoting a future for women's lives. I can also see how astute you were, in that Northern Ireland audiences didn't want to know about 'feminism'.

There is no doubt that we were feminists in the sense that we were presenting women, and very strong women, who always formed the centre of the plays, which were about empowering women. That's feminism. But at the time when Charabanc started (that was 1983) there were a lot of English theatre companies, trendy, middle-class and presenting feminism, and calling themselves feminists. It could be alienating and we were trying to encourage people to go to the theatre, people who had never been before, and we didn't want to put them off by having any kind of labels, we just wanted to say that this is a play about ordinary people.

When we started Charabanc we actually wanted a company of men and women but the irony is that most of the men were working and the women weren't. We didn't actually exclude men from the plays, we just played them ourselves and perhaps they appear quite stereotyped. But that's how all the women we interviewed saw their men, because there wasn't any great inter-action between men and women. The men didn't sit down and talk about their inner feelings.

Christina Reid talks about this, the total segregation of men and women. After Charabanc, you co-founded DubbelJoint Productions with artistic director Pam Brighton. What led to this coalition?

Pam had worked with Charabanc on a couple of plays in the early stages and then she went off to become a barrister and came back again. I had been doing some work with her in the BBC, where she was a drama producer. Pam and I had talked about a production for a festival, Belfast 1991. There was money sloshing around and we felt, wouldn't it be great to do something major, to bring together actors, directors, set designers and musicians, to bring the best of them all together and do something really really big and very very ambitious? (In retrospect, perhaps too ambitious, but you've got to be allowed to be able to do that, and make mistakes.)

There was great enthusiasm for *Hang All the Harpers*. We had the best musicians – Cathal Hayden, Sean O'Potts, Nollaig Casey, one of the McSharrys. We had myself and a wonderful team of actors, but it all became too ambitious. The whole project was a wonderful idea, just to map Irish culture, the language, the poetry from Elizabethan times right up to the present day and how it survived within a colonialist culture. It didn't really work – but I have never regretted doing it at all. Far more time and more editing would have helped, and I'm unsure of the wisdom of having two writers. Shane Connaughton was a writer at a distance and he was doing bits and I was doing bits, so that it felt just like that – far too 'bitty'. But that's why DubbelJoint started.

I did not want to get into that same kind of routine, play after play after play. I'm glad I did now, because I think it was *A Night in November* that came after that – no, it was *The Government Inspector*, which is still my favourite. But the next thing you do, you get locked into play to play to play, because now you have a production company, you now have staff, an administrator, an office, a business which you've got to keep going, so you do the next play. That's how DubbelJoint happened and why I had to continue – responsibility.

I thought Hang All the Harpers *was so different from anything we were used to, certainly in the Ulster theatre genre. But I did think that you didn't have proper time to cover that whole span of history and to hone it. None the less, it was an amazing achievement.* The Government Inspector, A Night in November *and* Stones in His Pockets *followed.*

Yes, the first production of *Stones* was up at Whiterock, in West Belfast.

To my mind it didn't work.

No, it didn't at all, and for a series of reasons. I didn't think the casting was right. It is very difficult to get those two characters right, they have to be right together, and I think I needed to do more work, I needed to edit it more, to rewrite it more. I think it needed more style, it didn't have a style – there wasn't any music, lights, sound, and this all adds to the whole atmosphere, the ambience of a piece. There are only two actors and in some plays you can get away with that, but here you were having to get people to imagine all sorts of different environments and I hadn't actually got it quite right in terms of the whole shape and movement of the play.

For instance, in the first production the character of Charlie starts talking about doing the film way early on and as the play progresses he adds more and more to the film so that it doesn't come as a surprise when they say, we can go and do this. It's much more interesting if he is internalising everything and suddenly states, just watch us, we can do this, and the audience goes, yeah you can! So that was a major thing that had to be taken out of the top of the play and changed to the end and then the whole finale changed. There's a much more upbeat ending.

And because each time they actually do a little sequence in the play, in the current production, the characters gain some power and are not as downtrodden as they actually were in the first production. I give them more scope. Also, the character of Sean Harkin has to appear so that the audience sees him and the reactions of Jake and Charlie to him, so that when they talk about his death at the end of the play we feel a loss shared.

It's a very brave thing to come back to a play that may not particularly have worked but you did – how come?

When David Grant was acting artistic director at the Lyric, he wanted to put something in at the end of the season and asked Ian McElhinney, my husband, and myself was there anything we would like to do together, and it was Ian's suggestion that he would love to do *Stones*, but to work with me to edit it, to rewrite it and to work with Conleth Hill, because it was written originally for him. That's how it happened and they did put a lovely shape and style to it that wasn't there before and I think it just needed that other 30 per cent of work from me also, to make it happen.

And maybe this is part of the problem that you had, working to deadlines on that sort of treadmill, which I don't think writers do any more, do they?

Well, I give *myself* a deadline, I don't mind giving myself one, but when it's imposed it's very difficult. I think the first one was imposed with *Stones* because we had to do the play before the end of the financial year, or place the company in jeopardy. So I thought, all right, I'll go ahead. I'm glad I did it, as, if I hadn't gone ahead, there wouldn't be *this Stones*, so everything is meant to be, for a reason.

We are leaping forward now to the revised Stones *and there hasn't been anything like its success. In Northern Ireland, we are so delighted for you, for the team, and you make us feel good by your success. Did you ever foresee this?*

No, no. I didn't at all. I knew that when we were doing it and I went round to rehearsal that there was something very special but I never thought that it would go to the West End, to Broadway, because, for me, the play defied all the West End rules, which, if there are any, would be related to names, stars. Somebody's got to be a name. Conleth, Sean [Campion] and me and Ian have been around here but are not known to a West End audience. The good thing was that we went on a journey and as the journey progressed, the word of mouth had built and built, long before any mention of the West End, never mind Broadway. We had toured and toured, to the Tricycle in London, back to Dublin, back to the Tricycle, to Edinburgh, to the Grand Opera House in Belfast, so that the play was a year going around and word of mouth building. By the time it got to the West End, it was actually called the Unstoppable Word of Mouth Hit. We went into a venue that does allow for … plays that are out there and making a bit of a name somewhere, which was the Ambassador, for twelve weeks, and then it was obvious that we had to move into a bigger venue in the West End, so hence the Duke of York and it's still there.

What about the whole business? You were used to being with a small independent theatre company, how did you manage the shift to the commercialism of the West End?

I have a very good agent, Ben Hall, who has been very careful about the plays because he knows me very well and he knows what we want and he is very protective. It's really down to him – he's done all the dealings. There are a lot of people involved now, it's not just me and Ian, and Sean and Conleth. There are investors and producers and all sorts of PR, press agents, and they are all in there as part of this huge industry. *Stones* is still running in London, it's just finished in Ireland, there's a world tour, it's in Vienna now, it's just come from Perth and then there's an American tour. It's on in Winnipeg, about to go to San Francisco, and that's all the one producer. The play has also been 'franchised', so there are other productions going on across the world. My agent keeps all this worry from my door.

And Ian has been directing Stones *in other countries, in Iceland, Finland, Sweden and Japan.*

That's because they have asked for him. There are a lot of countries which have the licence for the play and are just doing their own production, which is fine.

It was only a couple of years ago that Pam Brighton described DubbelJoint, after you had left (and the name connects Dublin and Belfast), as a nationalist company – which seemed strange, given the broad liberalism of your work.

It comes down to the same problem which we avoided with Charabanc. Once you label, you alienate. Plays speak for themselves. If a company or play is labelled, it will ostracise some of our community. The company is now run by Pam, and she has the right to label it, define it, as she sees appropriate. But my plays for the company could never be defined as nationalist or any other form of 'ism'.

It seems to me that all your plays are about people who are powerless and gain some kind of insight. Narrative and a powerful belief in humour inform the work. How do you shape the work in terms of form?

It varies. Sometimes I think there has been a form and a style that have been imposed on me because of the economics of theatre and I don't know if I could write a play with twelve characters, or thirteen or fourteen. Because I am so used to saying that I have three people here who can play everyone, I actually have to think that I can't have *that* person talking to *that* person because they are playing *that* person. They are playing both characters, so in a sense that restricts you, but it also is a good thing because it's discipline. In *Weddins, Weeins and Wakes*, which I rewrote for the Lyric, there are many characters but I have seven actors – very exciting with seven. There are times when you would love to have two of those characters talking to the two people they are playing, as that would make a really interesting theme but you can't have them seen together because they play the same people. In *A Night in November* it was fine because there was only one [actor]. Dan [Gordon] can play everyone, he can just do everything. But all the time you have to come back to [the character of] Kenneth McCallister, that's the only thing in a sense of form or style that is being imposed, and I have to think like that when I am writing.

Sometimes I will write out the story and then do the play. There's a road and there's a beginning and end but I know I have to get from the beginning to the end and this is the journey, this story. On the way you can go up here, stay here for another while and then you think, oh look, I can come round here and it's really interesting always knowing that you've got to get back to this point, and then there's all the meat and the texture, the depth and the substance, all these little alleyways here, and then when I look at all that, I have to have somebody come in like Ian ... A good director will map that out, make it happen on the page as well as on the stage. Then of course, the next step is when the actors come in and they take it further as well. That's how I work.

In that style it's very difficult to finish a play, to bring characters back to say, Well that's that now, folks, and out you go. You've journeyed so much that expectations are raised and there is no finite, satisfactory or easy ending to it all.

I think that's fine. That's life anyway, isn't it? In films it's different, the happy ending, having it all tied up. I think theatre people are much more open. In *HRT* there could have been an ending, and the audience expected that ending. When it didn't happen you could sense disappointment. In *Stones* everyone wants to know how Charlie and Jake are faring – that's theatre.

Belfast is important to your life and work. Given your success, you could live anywhere.

Belfast is the source of my material, every day out on the street talking and listening to people. It's about language. If I lived somewhere else, I couldn't hear these rhythms, how people verbalise their emotions, their humour, their anger. That's what I hear and write. And all my best friends live here.

Charabanc

A microcosm of the 'desperation' which led to the founding of the Northern Ireland Women's Rights Movement and, later, the NIWC, is evident within the founding principles of Charabanc Theatre Company. The company's history has been well documented, but it deserves summary and analysis within the framework of feminist/feminine theatre culture and by virtue of the company's own continual denial of a politically feminist perspective.

Charabanc was founded in 1983 by five actresses – Sarah (Marie) Jones, Eleanor Methven, Maureen McAuley, Carol Scanlan (later Moore) and Brenda Winter. They had become disillusioned by their own lack of professional employment opportunities and by their evaluation of the traditional theatre roles that existed for women – in their words, 'wives, mothers or the background for some guy on stage'. Again, in their words, 'the company was born out of frustration and boredom and the desire to do good work'.[1] The founding manifesto expressed commitment to 'presenting plays which reflect Northern Ireland society'.[2] Expressions of cultural or political objectives emerged stiltedly, and after their first productions. Charabanc began as 'a defiant gesture of self-help'.[3] Energy and self-determination were stronger hallmarks than intellectual or political vigour and the emergent formula of work was more informed by commitment to an ethos of social documentation within a vein of good craic, well and professionally executed, than by a sense of political or sociological ideology. If terms of reference were vague, allusions to feminism were consistently negative, although a commitment to writing the lives of women was paramount – in the words of the 1992 publicity brochure, 'putting women's experience to the fore'.

Their first piece was a depiction of women in the Belfast mills at the turn of the century, *Lay Up Your Ends*. The opening night at the Belfast Arts Theatre in May 1983 witnessed queues around the block and a reception that welcomed home Ulster theatre, depicting local lives and their histories, performed by local actresses. The work may have begun as an experimental act of faith but it ended up playing to 12,000 people. Charabanc's success continued with a similarly styled and informed version of life in Belfast during the 1949 election when, post-blitz, an emerging working-class politic of labour seemed hopeful. *Oul Delph and False Teeth* was first performed at the Arts Theatre, Belfast, in February 1984. This second production honed elements of socialist ideology and attempted to revise the given role of woman as subsidiary support to 'her man'. It now reads as though the influence of playwright Martin Lynch and his politics of non-sectarian socialism are central to themes and content, although there is some foregrounding, if not championing, of women.

Charabanc had yet to confirm its voice and stance and *Oul Delph and False Teeth* served as a transitional work, allowing the company to develop its links with communities and non-traditional venues. For their third collaborative work, Charabanc placed a group of women from a cross-section of the community in a residential reconciliation centre. *Now You're Talkin'*, first performed at the Arts Theatre in March 1985, focuses on contemporary women, their allegiances and, more importantly, their differences in terms of class and aspiration. This play witnesses the growing voice and identity of Marie Jones as writer, illustrates her ear for dialogue and demonstrates the beginning of a confidence in terms of collaborative textual structuring. But it is the production by Charabanc of a rural play which is crafted skilfully and moves with dramatic momentum that seals and identifies their vision. More particularly, the text places the company within the genre of an Ulster theatre tradition, representing the values of the earlier generation of

Ulster plays, set in the 1960s but written from the perspective of the mid-1980s.

The Girls in the Big Picture, first performed at the Ardhowen Theatre, Enniskillen, in September 1986, presents women within and across generations and, in so doing, would appear to highlight changing values and cultural attitudes.[4] The play is framed by two sets of spinsters, the old clichéd version of the two sisters in the country cottage (the Tuckey sisters), mirrored by the two young people, Margaret and Mary Jo, the spinsters-to-be, who have wished to fulfil small ambitions and have not entirely succeeded, who must compromise for the sake of survival and local dignity, a familiar story. Their ambition to open fancy coffee houses and fashion shops has been thwarted and their lives will be as unfulfilled as those of their predecessors. The Tuckey sisters win out in ensuring one marriage, a tentative one at that, with little real love on the part of the woman, but with economic salvation in securing ownership of the local Mace shop. Everyone else is left to their own devices, a younger generation volunteering a repetition in contemporary form of the lives and structures of the preceding generation, mostly a female way of living, alone or with each other, but focused on matriarchal control.

In *The Girls in the Big Picture* the norms of traditional Ulster theatre are respected. There is a modicum of narrative and plot development, and there is, most of all, the traditional tenacity of one couple, in this case women, outwitting another. We are reminded of the earlier Ulster comedies, where feuds, domestic and localised, are paraded centre stage. Charabanc's play endorses the historic matriarchy that has ruled kitchen hearths from generation to generation. In its text the older males have died and women's experiences are foregrounded. While adhering to the form of the traditional Ulster play, the company has highlighted gender roles with women at the centre.

In many ways this Charabanc play represents what Charabanc itself has represented to Northern Ireland. It is a well-crafted replica of a little part of Ulster society. The 'Basket Tea' ceremony, where a woman's basket of food is sold off to the highest bidder, with whom she must dance for the evening, represents ritualistic pairing without the nomenclature of the arranged wedding. It is a handy rural mechanism for otherwise awkward social situations. However, the ritual is not entirely successful, as the woman (Jean) who receives the highest bid takes matters into her own hands and makes her own decision on marriage. Such independence would have been unheard of in earlier texts. Matriarchal power replaces patriarchal authority.

The text of *The Girls in the Big Picture* has further ramifications. Since Charabanc and Field Day coexisted, sharing 'the big picture' of Ulster theatre throughout most of the 1980s and early 1990s,[5] obvious gender comparisons have been noted.[6] Almost binary opposition in terms of gendered founding membership is matched by opposing ideologies and methodologies. The hierarchical and intellectual base of one is challenged by the collaborative and intuitive operation of the other. Eleanor Methven comments on the generic differences between her company and Field Day:

> Field Day [was] formed ... on a very different basis, on an academic basis, on an aspiration of making a statement ... We came along from the other end of the spectrum. They had academic and literary heavyweights on their board, and we had local trade-union leaders and anybody who had been nice to us along the way ... But we were always praised for the rawness and the energy. There was just a slight edge of patronisation there.[7]

Most critical analyses of Charabanc are not text- or production-based, but rely on interviews with the central company members, Jones, Methven and Scanlan. While one critic may conclude that 'Charabanc always was its own best interpreter',[8] the company may have kept a few secrets to themselves. *The Girls in the Big Picture* could be read as a feminist antidote to Field Day's masculinity. The clever ambiguity of the title replaces the 'boys' of the big picture of Ulster theatre and, textually, women replace men as the real social activists. The setting of Cloughmartin is as Ulster and fundamentally Protestant as Friel's Ballybeg is Irish and Catholic. Field Day's intellectualism and ideology are contested by the dominant work ethic that informs *The Girls in the Big Picture*. And it is the women who slave away while Sidney slides out of his duties, chasing girls and fame as a country-and-western singer. There is a stunning parallel with the cameo love scene between Maire and Yolland in *Translations*[9] and between Margaret and Paul in *The Girls in the Big Picture*.[10] Where the former couple communicate without language, through gesture and intuition, the latter engage in a duel of dialogue and verbal innuendo, with Margaret winning the day. Friel's nostalgia for lost traditions in *Translations* is paralleled by generational contiguity in *The Girls in the Big Picture*. The values of one generation are passed to the next, while cultural changes – milk-shake machines, record players and deep-fat fryers – are purely superficial.

In many ways *The Girls in the Big Picture* allegorises Ulster theatre as a whole and Charabanc as a movement. Far from Field Day's fifth province of the imagination, Cloughmartin represents life as it was and is. We are very much in the province of Ulster and recall the founding manifesto of the ULT as dictated in *Uladh*: 'We have not striven to erect a barrier between Ulster and the rest of Ireland . . . If the result is provincial rather than national, it will not be our fault, but due to local influences over which we have no control.'[11]

This leads back to Charabanc's constant denial of the adjective 'feminist' being associated with its work. While some journalists have practically begged for approval of the ready and common assumption that Charabanc is a feminist company, a binary replacement of male with female does not in itself constitute a feminist ideology. Discussing the ritual of the 'greasing' of 'genitals' in *Lay Up Your Ends*, Helen Lojek summarises the point: 'The issue is power, not gender, and the play presents no idealised female world in which things are better when women are in charge.'[12] While Charabanc's work challenges the social marginalisation of women and women's issues, and celebrates 'the lives of women', there is almost a neurosis about the possibility of the company's own marginalisation if the term 'feminist' were adopted. Methven revealingly states: 'If we said we were feminist or socialist or any "ist" – it would completely alienate those people back in the community centres in Northern Ireland. So, what's the point of saying it?'[13] Here we have that hidden feminist consciousness, which, if revealed, would indeed 'alienate' Ulster audiences.

The point is accentuated by Methven earlier in 1986 to the *Boston Globe*, whose reporter comments that Charabanc's women do not 'see themselves as a militantly feminist company'. The American reporter's disappointment highlights cultural difference and the absurdity of equating American feminist politics with those of Northern Ireland in the 1980s. Methven responds: 'We don't want to start that sort of war here, of all places.'[14] Within the conservatism of Ulster politics, it was politically expedient and astute to deny suggestions of political radicalism or radical feminism. With aims of mainstream acceptance, perhaps a remark by Harris proposes another agenda: 'The company existed,' she says, 'because they had a vision of their dramatic futures and worked hard to realise it.'[15]

So Charabanc cannot be accused of *not* being what they never *meant* to be. In 1992 they listed as the first of three 'strands' to their work 'devising plays from and primarily for the community in which we live'. That is exactly what they achieved and their legacy will be the reintroduction of an authentic Ulster voice and an authentically Ulster theatre, radical in so doing but as non-feminist as the society they replicated. It could not be anything else if that first strand of their policy was to be realised. The dark nights of the 1970s in Belfast were not conducive to theatre-going or theatre production. Charabanc's courageous venture may have led to the rise of young independent theatre companies in the late 1980s and 1990s – Tinderbox, Big Telly and later Mad Cow, now, in PC speak, Prime Cut. However, I remember the work for its high production values and performances which were outstanding. These standards were brought to community centres, to day centres and to leisure centres across Northern Ireland, the relevance of the themes appealing to young and old. Charabanc revived a belief in the production of theatre in the North and became a legend in its own time – if all those who claim to have seen *Lay Up Your Ends* actually did see it, it might still be running.

But quality alone could not sustain the company and when Marie Jones departed in 1990 the company's identity, and indeed its loyal community audience, started to dissolve. There was a sense of floundering in the choice of material: Darragh Cloud's *The Stick Wife*, Neil Speirs's *Cauterised*, Federico García Lorca's *The House of Bernarda Alba*. I contend Christopher Murray's suggestion that Charabanc's 'demise in 1995 was surely premature'.[16] The company had lost its appealing identity and had drifted from its original purpose. Charabanc had become like any other theatre company and the tenth-anniversary party in May 1993 loudly stated the changed ideology when Methven, Scanlan and Stella McCusker (a well-known actress who had joined the company for *Bernarda Alba*) appeared in lavish ball-gowns.

The dress code may have represented an elaborate joke but the roots of community concern and working–class allegiance seemed to have dissolved, as the members, understandably, sought roles within the broader context of Irish theatre.

If Marie Jones's departure was Charabanc's loss, it was to her own creative gain as playwright. The constant, collaborative need to write 'of and for the community' had sometimes been criticised as non-creative and indeed exploitative of the very communities the work was intended to serve. Freed from the essential literalness of the 'then' and 'now' of Ulster life, Jones could develop themes and forms more readily based on the concept of 'what if', operating in the subjunctive territory of the imagination and creating the possibility of imagined futures, an impossibility within the given policy and commitment of Charabanc.

Marie Jones with Charabanc

The textual legacy of Jones is significant and one text in particular, *Somewhere Over the Balcony*, evidences Charabanc's by now sophisticated insight of a community turned upside down by violence. It also represents a formal creativity which has been achieved by Jones. In terms of Ulster theatre *Somewhere Over the Balcony* mirrors the 1969 anarchy of form and content in John Boyd's *The Flats*. Boyd's quotidian mayhem has been updated by Jones and his inversion of normality has become Northern Ireland's norm.

Somewhere Over the Balcony is set in the nationalist Divis Flats complex, a stone's throw, literally, from Boyd's loyalist Unity Flats, and, twenty years on, another kind of stone's throw from the apparently absurd chaos represented by Boyd. It is a chaos that, in *Somewhere Over the Balcony*, has become institutionalised within its community, a living culture whose socially incongruous codes and standards have been communally ratified. The mania of *The Flats* is positively low-key in comparison to the breathless antics of *Somewhere Over the Balcony*.

Three women, Kate Tidy, Ceely Cash and Rose, share a 'normal' day high up on the balcony of the last remaining tower block of Divis Flats. If the image suggests isolation, loneliness and boredom, their reality is far from it. A wedding party turns into a riot – 'the best dressed riot I've ever seen', remarks Kate. The guests are held under siege in the chapel, forty-five chicken salads are ordered while guests play bingo and children climb the statues. Meanwhile, the female trio on the balcony is under its usual army surveillance from the fifteenth floor. There is a controlled explosion and Kate's worst nightmare of the walls of her flat caving in becomes reality. A 'dole snooper' (official from the Department of Health and Social Services), disguised as a British Army paratrooper, is caught by one of the many Tuckers; there is the continuous washing of cars without engines (kept looking good 'in case the hoods steal them'); and an ambulance and a helicopter are hijacked. Collectors' items, relics of the conflict, including the first bin lid of internment morning, are catalogued for sale to foreign journalists. (At 4 am on the morning of Monday 9 August 1971 the Army raided the houses of alleged IRA suspects to arrest them under the Special Powers Act. Subsequently the women banged bin lids to warn the community of the approach of the British Army troops.)

Males, young or old, are named 'Tucker', a pet name for Thomas, but, according to Marie Jones, used consistently in the text to suggest the alliterative effect of the constant *tuc tuc tuc* of overhead British Army surveillance helicopters. Young Tucker is on voluntary work experience, guarding an empty tower block which is haunted by the ghosts of 'two glorious Gloucesters', members of an earlier British Army surveillance team. The disguised dole snooper tries to apprehend him. Granda Tucker, who has refused to speak since internment, hijacks the helicopter and declares, 'Attention, the enemy, this is Commanding Officer ... Tucker Allouisis Cash of the 21st Ardoyne Battalion.'[17] This Tucker's exploits are crowned by another Tucker, who is not Tucker, who is Tootsie:

> ROSE: The best man does not look like himself.
> CEELY: That's because he is not himself.
> ROSE: Who is he?
> CEELY: Tootsie O'Hare disguised as Big Tucker O'Neill.
> ROSE: Where is Big Tucker O'Neill?
> KATE: On the run disguised as Tootsie O'Hare.
> ROSE: Why?
> CEELY: Cos Danny didn't want Tucker, he wanted Tootsie.

KATE: So Tootsie is Tucker and Tucker is Tootsie!

ROSE: Why is Tucker on the run when he didn't do nothing?

CEELY AND KATE: So Tootsie could be best man, for fuck's sake.

ROSE: Right![18]

These absurdities posing as logic pile up on each other, until little Dustin, whose destiny has already been sealed by not having been named Tucker, becomes a social outcast because he is doing well at school and wants to become a computer scientist:

CEELY: I'm all excited so I am ... when wee Tucker was wee, big Tucker used to say to him, 'Son what do you wanna be when you grow up', and he woulda said, 'On the run, Daddy.' Oh God if he was alive the day he would be so proud of him ... he's probably in Bundoran by now.

KATE: (upset) It's well for you Ceely, my Dustin wants to become a computer scientist.

CEELY: My wee Tucker was just lucky, Kate, he happened to be in the right place at the right time.[19]

All the Tuckers are as remote from the women's emotional or sexual interest as the surveillance squaddies on the roof. The real hero worship is reserved for the canine vigilantes, Pepe and Rambo McGlinchey. They achieve true acts of heroism simply because they are there and not on the run. Pepe and Rambo are the real custodians of Divis Flats and protect its inhabitants from all outside forces. The two dogs have survived plastic bullets and whatever else to protect their community.

At the end of Act 1 Kate announces, 'On a day like today, you could be anywhere.'[20] This relentless comic roll of inversion depicts a community that is well past a form of madness. It has settled more than comfortably into it, a chronic form of institutionalised insanity. While Boyd in his *Flats* demonstrated the early symptoms, Jones, in hers, presents the long-term outcome. How is this received by community audiences whose lives are comically paraded as abnormal and close to madness? Jones incorporates all the elements of traditional comic form. Inversion operates throughout and the controlling factor of laughter accentuates the ambiguity of reception. This is not laughter *with*, and it is not entirely laughter *at*. It is a resigned laughter, together with a desperate acceptance of life which acknowledges complete powerlessness. There is no notion here of McGuinness's psychic journeys towards redemption or Reid's expedient emigrations. In fact, the only journey will be as far as the Falls Road, and that does not necessitate getting out of slippers and dressing gown.[21]

Somewhere Over the Balcony forges a meta-reality, a world of illusion, which is the world of comedy. The difference is that there is no reversion to normality. The comic world of inversion is sustained and the changed perceptions, which are the expected norm of comedy, do not occur. Perceptions remain steadfast and the inversion never reverts. If the illusion of comic form opens the text, there is no re-establishment of order to close it. Illusion and inversion persist and are sustained and ingrained by the annunciation of the refrain, 'On a day like today, you could be anywhere.' There is a congruence of form and content. The kaleidoscope of activity presented by the invented lives of the three women is matched by their hallucinations, their invention of life and lives around them. The voyage of discovery, through comedy's inversion, becomes a voyage of confirmation and reinforcement.

While the trio embarks on an excursion of invention and inversion, the women never return from it. There is an exhausted pause after all the exhilaration. Tomorrow there may not be a wedding, but the Tuckers, the dogs, the useless cars, the empty tower blocks, the surveillance squaddies, and Kate, Ceely and Rose will be there to start the whole business all over again. Like every morning, Kate Tidy will sit, Beckett-like, on her galvanised bin and talk to herself about life and reality as she sees it from the balcony. Life in Divis Flats has become one unending comedy. Edith Kern describes a similar scenario: 'The morality prevailing is that of the oppressed, not the rulers, and their liberating laughter belongs to the realm of the imaginary.'[22] There is no liberation for these women, and Jones simply finds ways in which they may respectfully enfranchise themselves within a micro-society from which they are totally disenfranchised. Their limited power is imaginary. But it is more real than their four walls, which cave in. Their power of imagination translates turmoil, poverty and emotional absence into their opposites. As Kern states: 'It is the fantasy triumph of the meek and powerless over those in authority.'[23]

Here, Jones stage-manages an audience into a reluctant critical posture. It is uneasy. The image of a section of society on stage confronts the audience with its own backyard. The safe stock responses of Ulster theatre are challenged. There is no easy acquiescence or acceptable formulas. Neither is there an empathy, because the lives and contexts are too far removed, too dramatically manic, to elicit normal responses. Perhaps the response is a sense of guilt, an unquiet feeling that we are all responsible and impotent. Certainly, the safety of the comic form becomes positively the opposite and challenges its own norms in *Somewhere Over the Balcony*. The play opened immediately after the Remembrance Sunday bombing in Enniskillen, County Fermanagh, in November 1987.[24] The company contemplated cancellation but, in theatrical tradition, went on with the show at the Belfast Arts Theatre. For the audience that week there was a mixed response, built from complex allegiances and the immediacy of more suffering because of the bombing. I feel that this wonderful play was not given an opportunity in Northern Ireland − as so often, awful circumstances overshadowed the work.

This text represents a watershed, however, a keen understanding and endorsement of the Charabanc ethos, 'from and for the community'. It also represents the height of creativity within that vein of naturalism and reality and converts both integral features into their opposites. The borderlines between the surreal and the real, between sanity and madness, are totally blurred. For Marie Jones as playwright, this text may have presented the challenge, the kind of possibilities, she would confront within differing modes and forms in the future.

While Charabanc worked across communities, another text by Marie Jones, *Weddins, Weeins and Wakes*, emerged from a Protestant community and for the Shankill Festival in 1989. (*Weddins* was rewritten by Jones and revived by the Lyric Threatre in November 2001.) The quotidian reality of one community (Divis Flats) is mirrored by its next-door neighbour across a few Belfast streets. In Jones's Protestant community, economics of existence, community peer pressure and an absence of any integration of the sexes or love by, with or for anyone are shared with the text that portrays Catholic communal life in *Somewhere Over the Balcony*. Emotional life has little space within cultures where the external trappings of impoverished living are paraded; pawn shops are replaced by mail order catalogues, OK Taxis drive the bride (Wendy) to the church, as she fantasises that she is marrying rock star Robbie Williams as opposed to Ulster Volunteer Force (UVF) foot soldier Derek McNeill, who turns up for the wedding drunk and dishevelled. Pigeons are more important than people and Wendy threatens to phone the UVF to have them executed before her wedding.

Watching the Watson family preparing for the wedding and watching every other move on the street are Mona and Molly, who are themselves 'watched'. Mona has laid out the dead and enjoyed good wakes all her life, while Molly has been midwife to a whole community – 'I've delivered half of them Orangemen.'[25] Their redundant roles allow for reminiscence and the continual 'watch' and commentary. As in *Somewhere Over the Balcony*, there is an almost Beckett-like scene where Molly and Mona, not 'walking',[26] are left bereft and isolated outside their front doors. Life is at its lowest ebb without gossip or focus:

> MOLLY: What will we do, for we're up that early
> We have a clatter more hours to fill?
>
> MONA: Sure if we just let on it's later than it is
> Then it won't seem as long as until
>
> MOLLY: But if we let on now what about later?
>
> MONA: When we think it's the time that it's not
> Then we'll think it's earlier than we thought.
>
> MOLLY: So what yer saying is if we just pretend
> They'll be back round about eight
> But it will only be six and nobody here.

In her reversals of reality, Jones performs another coup. Since Belfast business will be closed down for the Twelfth, there is neither an undertaker to lay out grandfather Archie, nor a taxi to get Wendy to the City Hospital to give birth. Molly and Mona are back in business.

The snapshot of *Weddins, Weeins and Wakes* depicts everyone sniping at everyone else. Political ideology is as far removed from this world as the idea of Robbie Williams marrying Wendy. Archie's sash is not allowed to adorn his body 'for the worms to eat', but is draped over the new baby. Like *Somewhere Over the Balcony*, pigeons, dogs, and unusable cars are given more attention than human beings. These are the facts of life, where paraphernalia and gossip are more important to economic survival than the politics of the conflict. A code of mercenary one-upmanship, which parallels social legitimacy without participating in its accountability, is the dream of all of these characters. Mona and Molly will sell out Eddie without thought or concern and, over the way in Divis Flats, Kate, Rose and Ceely will battle out their individual paths to fortune, depending on who owns the real internment morning bin lid. Jones's invention of a bizarre universe, inhabited by three women in *Somewhere Over the Balcony* and depicted by Molly and Mona's enclosed lives in *Weddins, Weeins and Wakes*, is testimony to the power of her imagination and creative ability, which had to develop beyond the realm of fact and history.

In 1991 Jones and former Charabanc director Pam Brighton founded DubbelJoint Productions. As the name suggests, the policy was to tour relevant work north and south of the border and to employ the best theatre professionals from the two territories. Given the joint efforts by the two Arts Councils to liaise on practical programmes, the founding ideology was timely and appropriate. There was no overt political exponent as such, until much later when Jones had parted company with Brighton and the founding ideology was suddenly revised to state that DubbelJoint 'was formed to fill a niche for nationalist plays'.[27]

DubbelJoint's ideology does not seem entirely congruent with that of Jones, who in her work definitively searches for a cultural freedom, but one which is beyond the environs of nationalism, unionism, Protestantism or Catholicism, and certainly beyond the prerogative of male or female. The journeys that inform the essential feminism of McGuinness operate to an extent in *Hang All the Harpers*, *Stones in His Pockets*, *A Night in November* and *Women on the Verge of HRT*. Liberation is the informing movement and theme, and it is cross-gender and cross-community. Closed and colonial values are criticised, whether they belong to one political or gender camp or the other.

While there is truth in Charabanc's claim to represent both communities, it is a reflection of Northern Ireland's polarity that its texts reflect that polarity unless it has been consciously removed, as in *Now You're Talkin'* (set in a reconciliation centre), or *Gold in the Streets*, which deals with the effects of emigration. In 1990 for the Belfast Festival at Queen's, Charabanc presented a double bill featuring *Weddins, Weeins and Wakes* and *The Blind Fiddler of Glenadauch*, a critique of the values of the aspiring middle-class Catholic community. This double bill entertained festival audiences but notably did not tour to the communities which had seen one play or the other, but never both. It would seem that Jones had tired of such polarity and its constant representation.

Her first play for DubbelJoint was *Hang All the Harpers*,[28] a collaboration with novelist Shane Connaughton. The broad historical sweep and formal style reflect the Charabanc ethos while tackling a theme and history beyond immediate community borderlines. The play represents a cultural challenge to masculine linear history. Two women and a dog become the narrators of revisionism, and music becomes the bonding ideology, which is free from religion, gender or politics. In contemporising society within this text, Jones makes her first move at cross-community gesturing. Her character Colin lives in the Protestant Waterside area of Derry and watches as proceedings for a community theatre open-air celebration of the siege[29] occur in the Guildhall Square on the Derry side of the river, where the population, and, it is assumed, most of the participants in the siege play, are Catholic. The narrative is based on an actual theatrical event which had been organised by Derry City Council in 1991. As well as the name change from Londonderry City Council to the perceived nationalist nomenclature of Derry City Council, the play was also perceived to constitute a hijacking of Protestant culture by the Catholic-dominated council. Colin's wife, Pauline, thinks he is completely mad when he decides to cross the bridge and participate in the celebrations, perceived by her to be a triumphal affirmation of the real everyday siege 'by taigs'. That Colin ventures with his Lambeg drum across the divide is Jones's attempt at the kind of reality which was impossible to achieve within Charabanc. It is, however, a complicated reality and one which is never fully resolved. The colonisation of music in *Hang All the Harpers* is depicted by Thomas Moore's recitals in the drawing rooms of the colonisers. Ironically, the final truth may indeed belong to Pauline, that Derry Catholics *have* colonised the original colonisers, their Protestant ancestry. The Thomas Moore metaphor may have been inverted and updated.

Narrator Rose is allowed a freedom of conviction which belongs to her outsider status. The narrator device itself opens the text and absolves closure. Her ironic message at the end of the penultimate scene becomes, finally, another kind of message. She says, 'We are the music makers. We are the makers of dreams.' But it is not clear that this conviction has been dramatically realised. The final assertion of celebration of song and music belongs to Rose alone and apparently is Jones's statement to the audience:

> ROSE: God love them ... they are the ones locked up in souless boxes ... we are free, Martha ... and we can still sing from our souls ... the soul of our bards ... the soul that they tried to make me ashamed of, God help them.[30]

To sing is to be free but that freedom is not a prerogative and is as open to colonisation as any other construct. While Martha and Rose wander free, there is another code operating for the rest of their society.

Endings are never easy for Jones, perhaps a legacy of the Charabanc days when the very notion of closure was synonymous with 'making a statement'. Charabanc, according to Jones at the time, was 'frightened about making a statement', frightened that 'people would say, "Ah, that's what Charabanc thinks, that's a statement."' This fear on the part of a challenging theatre company is difficult to comprehend. Has a desire to please the audience become the guiding force? In *Hang All the Harpers*, Rose's is the authorial voice and the apolitical stance of a song or of traditional music is seen as the true embodiment of cultural freedom, endorsed and enshrined by Jones. The concept is often repeated, in different ways, in future texts.

In *A Night in November*,[31] Colin of *Hang All the Harpers* is replaced by Kenneth McCallister. The World Cup replaces Derry's siege celebrations and football replaces the unifying force of music. Like Pauline, Kenneth's wife, Debrah, is left alone with her bigotry and social self-interest. She is more concerned about her husband's future as a member of the golf club than in the politics of Northern Ireland. Pauline, Debrah and their Catholic counterpart in *The Blind Fiddler of Glenadauch* all engage in an endorsement of social ladder climbing, of 'getting on in life'. They are portrayed as endorsers and custodians of the patriarchal world that has imprisoned them, the female versions of the colonised who have become the colonisers.

The interrogation of Protestantism as patriarchy becomes genderless. Its equation with power, personal stultification and social fixity is challenged by men, Colin and Kenneth McCallister. Catholicism is represented as liberation, joy and fluidity, all concepts which Anne Devlin will portray as being denied within that culture. The version of Catholic culture as presented in *A Night in November* is as clichéd as it is untrue. We are expected to believe that because the home of Kenneth's Catholic colleague is ramshackle, untidy and disorganised life is somehow wonderful for its Catholic inhabitants. They read books and go to the pictures, when, according to Protestant ethics, they should be cooking meals for their husbands and cleaning the house. If this is the liberation the Women's Movement fought so hard for, then it is a sad day for feminism and, indeed, for theatre in Northern Ireland. While there may be truth in cliché, there may also be naïveté in its presentation.

Kenneth's subsequent voyage of liberation with 'Jack's Army' to the World Cup Finals in the United States is dramatically credible due to the mania and speed of the reversals and narration of the one-person-show format. An audience believes that staid Kenneth, husband, father and a dole clerk, whose sole ambition is to become a member of the golf club, may cross sectarian boundaries to a world of cultural liberation which is based on football matches and perpetual drunkenness. It is a patriarchal world, whether Protestant or Catholic, and the representation of Kenneth's 'liberation' remains dubious. Football may be preferable to golf, and Catholics may seem more easygoing than Protestants, while the cultural constructs that govern Northern Ireland have hardly been dissected. But it was the kinetic presentation and superb performance by Dan Gordon as Kenneth that made *A Night in November* a theatrical experience. The truth of cliché becomes apparent and Kenneth becomes a metaphor of political possibilities. The suspension of disbelief is paramount.

The title *Women on the Verge of HRT*[32] suggests analysis of a female condition and attracts audiences by the suggestion of a single gendered exposition of that condition. The play, first produced in August 1995 at the Belfast Institute of Further and Higher Education, Whiterock Road, Belfast, deals with levels of fantasy and illusion, which Jones removes from a masculine world of logic and reason. The text is deliberately loose on logic, while its technical strengths control a world of comic inversions, fantasies, contradictions and opposites. The single reality that fading female beauty is not attractive to men of an equal age opens and very nearly closes the text, before another inversion operates. Like *Somewhere Over the Balcony*, the final reconciliation and restoration of order are disrupted by another gesture of defiance. The traditional happy ending, of marriage within comic form, becomes its opposite, separation – a contemporary liberation perhaps.

Anna and Vera are on their annual pilgrimage from Belfast to singer Daniel O'Donnell's tea party in Kincasslagh, County Donegal. The play opens with an optional video recording of Anna and Vera in the queue with hundreds of other women to be greeted by the man himself, who remembers *their* names, as he does the many others, and his actual presence both re-inforces and subverts the fantasy element of the pilgrimage. Removed from everyday reality, another form of romantic reality is materialised by O'Donnell's actual touching of the pilgrims. It is this gesture that obsesses Anna throughout Act 1. Dreams may become reality and, indeed, have done during the afternoon. In the bedroom of O'Donnell's hotel, The Viking, Anna settles for the night with an effigy of his face on her pillowcase. She opens a large romantic novel. Vera settles for a large vodka and a tirade against her former husband, Dessie, who has married Susie, twenty-five years younger and mother of his first son. Vera has had four daughters and the birth of a son is seen as the renewal of virility and a downgrading of Vera's abilities. As Vera struts, chain-smoking and ordering vodkas from the bar downstairs, Anna tries to convince her that her own life is fine with husband Marty, although it emerges that they no longer sleep together. Fergal, the night porter, is regularly summoned. He is a surrogate Daniel, providing more comic inversion. While he indulges in the practical pretence that the visitors are high on lemonade and mixers, he attends to their emo-tional fantasies, singing songs of love and hope and telling them that they are spiritually and deeply lovable. He invites Vera to watch the dawn.

For Fergal, the dawn is a time of silent wishes and dreams materialising – he is a magician who can make lit cigarettes disappear and women's dreams come true. The background male figures are summoned and Dessie and Marty, as well as Dessie's new wife, in varying ways confirm the truth of Vera's conviction that older women are for the scrap heap. Some home truths about Vera are also revealed, particularly that she did not love Dessie.

But the most startling revelation is that both Anna and Marty have secretly colluded in lives of fantasy and over a long period of time. There is no communication as the pair indulge in separate occupational therapies – Anna in romantic novels and Daniel's songs, Marty in pornography. The biological and cultural isolation Vera has described throughout the text becomes a shared isolation and a mutual pact of silent acceptance and despair in the lives of Anna and Marty.

Fergal, porter-magician, has done a disappearing act while encounters have occurred. He returns to quote poetry, kiss Vera and disappear in a puff of stage smoke. His presence is as real and allusive as that of Daniel O'Donnell, real in its manifestation as porter in The Viking hotel (as Daniel's kissing of the pilgrims in the introductory video) and unreal in his convenient disappearing act post magic tricks to bring characters to meet Vera and Anna. Only memories and songs may compensate for the 'real thing' – the meeting with Daniel and the dawn encounter with Fergal – and both become interwoven, fact and fantasy conducting everyday lives. In turn, Jones has introduced parallel mechanisms to match those of the present and absent characters (Daniel and Fergal, both reconciled as 'present' in the minds of Anna and Vera, and, of course, in the minds of the audience).

The song of the finale is almost in protest at all that has happened, the inversions and truths, the fictions and facts, and is designed to send an audience off with a warm glow, despite the revelations to the contrary:

> We are women on the verge
> And we won't take ignorin'
> No sex hospice for us
> We are still up to scoring
> So come on sisters
> Don't let them win
> We may be over forty
> But we can still sin, sin, sin.[33]

This ending is as much a mirage as the carefully constructed details that came before. The factual exposition is that Anna's life, carefully romanticised and therefore protected, has been shattered. We are encouraged simply to comply with the closure, non-feminine and didactic, to celebrate some kind of dubious victory that has hardly been demonstrated by the text.

Stones in His Pockets has been a commercial success in the West End; an earlier version of the play was performed at the Belfast Institute of Further and Higher Education, Whiterock Road, Belfast, for the West Belfast Festival in August 1996. The original production by DubbelJoint passed without much comment. At the time I wrote, 'The writing is at a faster pace than material or formal structuring can allow.' Indeed, when David Grant and Ian McElhinney decided to reproduce the show as an end-of-year popular slot for the Lyric Theatre's season in 1999, the choice did not seem inspired. Employing two actors, the decision seemed to be more based on economics than art. How wrong can one be? Rewritten by Jones and with McElhinney's direction of Conleth Hill and Sean Campion as Charlie and Jake, this production leapt with theatricality.

The extraordinary imaginative form Jones employed in *Somewhere Over the Balcony* and the sheer theatricality of *A Night in November* reach a creative apex in *Stones in His Pockets*. Kenneth McCallister's character changes are multiplied when Charlie and Jake transcend themselves during a Hollywood shoot for 'The Quiet Land' in Kerry. The pair are extras on a forty-pound-a-day shoot, watched over by Mickey, a kind of extra supremo who learnt his trade on *The Quiet Man*.

In Jones's rewriting, textual explanations in lengthy dialogue between Charlie and Jake become dramatised and subtextual, with the pair more often 'others' than themselves. The text becomes more dramatic and less explanatory as the invented characters take over from those of Charlie and Jake and take on real lives of their own – the genius of Jones is her constant reinventions. The frenetic multiplication and interchange of character and gender create a headlong dramatic momentum. The pair's tendency to indulge in angst is disrupted and shifted to the end of the play. In turn, Charlie's Northern male reticence is underlined. The cultural distance between masculine North and a more open feminine South parallels the central focus of cultural intrusion by the big Hollywood production team. Charlie's hay fever is an excuse for more metaphorical reasons and, through Jake's interrogation, it emerges that, like Sean Harkin, Charlie has attempted suicide but 'couldn't even do that right'. Charlie and Jake decide to make their own movie, calling it 'Stones in His Pockets' – in other words, the true story. Clem, director of the sham 'The Quiet Land', expresses Jones's comic perspective:

> How many people want to see a film about a suicide? People want happy endings. Life is tough enough. People don't go to the movies to get depressed.[34]

Neither do 'people' attend Jones's plays 'to get depressed'. Clive Barnes in the *New York Post*, after the first night of *Stones in His Pockets* on Broadway (1 April 2001), could be writing about *Weddins, Weeins and Wakes* when he says that Jones has 'a priceless sense of the absurd, and can spin a tale with dizzying speed ... with the dauntless ease of a champion ice-skater on thin ice and beguilingly drunk'. When the plays' affirmative finales posit closure (*Women on the Verge of HRT*, *Hang All the Harpers*) and the songs and music disguise exposition, there is a definite sense of 'thin ice', and Barnes is right to employ the analogy with admiration. In *Stones in His Pockets*, Clem is caricatured for obtuse handling of what Jones achieves with distinction – the aftermath of the Hollywood glow. Future realities are denied contemplation as characters whose lives are perhaps, in reality, grounded disappear into a theatrical sunset.

While Charlie and Jake's dreams arise from human concerns in *Stones in His Pockets*, Molly and Mona's in *Weddins, Weeins and Wakes* are firmly based on the economic principle. Their business plan centres on exploitation, imitation brass from the market at Nutt's Corner further reduced down in quality for cheap coffin handles and 'chape wood' to imitate solid oak. Jones portrays a myopia within which the possibility of cultural identities embracing each other is remote. Life is portrayed at its most basic and engraved in the values underpinning Molly and Mona's funeral parlour/birth clinic. Yet the mania of all these texts is controlled and presented by a unique technique. Though small casts may originally have been an economic necessity, *Stones in His Pockets* transcends the limitation to create an art form. As in *Somewhere Over the Balcony*, literal and metaphorical worlds are presented through the medium of a single actor, or two or three. There are good monologues in contemporary theatre, but nothing to match this level of sophistication, where the minimalist writing on the page can explode into such a theatrical display.

It is Jones's understanding of theatre production and her consciousness of the collective that has informed her recent writing and rewrites. The subordination of text to production is unusual and upsets critics. Ben Brantley in the *New York Times* was 'thrilled' by *Stones in His Pockets*, but had to say that the play was 'less literary than kinetic', a pertinent statement. The kinetic is central to the writing and it is Jones's triumph that she signals more than she states in her recent work. Subverting dominant forms of theatre and, in particular, the Irish literary pastoral tradition, Jones presents an urban metaphysical claustrophobia. *Weddins, Weeins and Wakes* is also based on, built around and generated by kinetic energy. She may skate as long as she wishes over *very* 'thin ice', but in this play, with a cast and production team who represent the best in Ulster theatre, including herself and two Charabanc founders, Eleanor Methven and Carol Moore, McElhinney's direction and Trevor Moore's musical composition, the 'ice' is likely to hold.

In *Somewhere Over the Balcony*, *Hang All the Harpers*, *A Night in November*, and *Women on the Verge of HRT*, form allows and, indeed, implements the inversions of Shakespearean comedy. However, these do not reach formal conclusions in reconciliation. Instead, they seem to omit a stage in the process. Individual freedom leaves behind it a real world of stagnation, one which is even more entrenched in its myopia than before the individual's departure from it. While Colin (*Hang All the Harpers*) and Kenneth (*A Night in November*) may leave one tribe to join another, Vera and Anna (*Women on the Verge of HRT*), as middle-aged women, do not have a tribe to join. The audience is exhorted to celebrate membership of a female tribe which depends on 'scoring' and not letting the opposition 'win', a conundrum at best.

What Jones may lose in the credibility of closure is championed by her use of dialogue. Its sharp, caustic wit undermines pretension and accentuates an authentic Belfast voice. It is this very authenticity and the textual replication of it that present Jones with formal difficulties – how to bring characters back after experience away (her comic inversions), how to harmonise lives within a broader spectrum, how to convince that individual voyages have collective relevance. *Somewhere Over the Balcony* is a comic theatrical excursion and maps the social and political hegemonies of Northern Ireland. Coherence is attempted but not fully realised in later texts, which move beyond the environs of geographical areas and issues into, ironically, a more overt landscape of ideology: *Hang All the Harpers, A Night in November, Women on the Verge of HRT* and, to an extent, *Stones in His Pockets. Weddins, Weeins and Wakes* reverts to, and was written as part of, an earlier formula of replication and dramatic representation, although the kinetic principle spectacularly dominates and controls the blank verse of the revised script.

None the less, the comic form has satisfied creative exigency for Jones. That articulation may never espouse woman as independent subject, but it may create a more balanced voice within Northern Ireland theatre. Jones is striving towards a form that liberates. There is a confusion, contradiction even, between the textual facts, the objective realities which deny liberation and the playwright's desire for it. In a very real sense, Marie Jones envisages futures that are sometimes beyond her characters' imaginings.

4 Christina Reid
In the company of women

Interview with Christina Reid, June 2002

Your childhood in Belfast seems to have had a powerful influence on your work, so can you tell me something more about those years?

I was brought up in two houses, my parents' house in the Ardoyne and my maternal grandparents' house on the Donegall Road. The women's lives revolved around the children and the home. The men had an outside life – work, the pub, the bookies, football matches. And every July, when my granny rented a house in Donaghadee, the men stayed in Belfast during the week and came down at the weekends and for the Twelfth fortnight. In their absence, the women were different. More relaxed, bawdier, full of life and banter.

So the gender dichotomy was very strong, with the women separate from the men for periods of time (but not all the time)?

That's right. Granny's clan was predominantly female and much of my growing up was spent in the company of generations of aunts, daughters, sisters, cousins. The boys were a part of this group until they were old enough to join the men in their separate life outside the home. The women ran everything, but there was a saying among them: 'Men need to think they're the boss of the duck.' In other words, let them think they're in charge.

What influenced you to write – an unusual activity?

My mother had a great thing about reading. She got us library tickets, books from the library – she couldn't afford to buy them. I ended up getting on her nerves because I was reading and not doing the housework with her. I loved stories, the beginning, middle and end, so I started writing my own in one of those padded five-year diaries which came with a lock and key. I made them very melodramatic. Again, that comes from the verbal storytelling that went on in the family. My grandmother and her sisters were *seanchaí* without knowing it. They weaved fact and fiction, created huge scenarios and also they acted them out, dressed up, and danced and sang as if they were in the Hollywood movies. There would be a grain of recognisable truth and then winding improvisation. I imitated the technique in my versions in my five-year diary.

When did you 'come out', as it were, as a writer, because it must have been before you went to Queen's as a mature student?

In 1980 I wrote a play for a UTV competition and won the Thames Television Award. Later I was invited to become writer in residence at the Lyric Theatre. By then I was a mature student at Queen's and a single parent. Unfortunately something had to give and it was university, which I'm sorry about because I enjoyed it so much.

To move on to the plays, I'm really interested in how you deal with generations and history, and that all probably comes from the family.

It comes from that big family and the generations who were there together. I had heard the stories so many times that I knew them as if I was there when they happened. I actually had a picutre in my head of them and I could remember seeing the people and I could see it happening, so I think that's where the stage writing emerged from, the visual memories.

There is an ambivalence in that you depict different versions of history. You have a huge respect on the one hand, it seems, but you are also interrogating, like Frank McGuinness in Observe the Sons of Ulster Marching Towards the Somme. *He brings the men to the brink but they cannot reinvent their allegiances.*

My grandfather was like that. When I asked him about the Somme he talked about valour, patriotism, loyalty. He wouldn't question it. He couldn't, because to question the war would have meant questioning his peacetime allegiances too, King and Country, God and Ulster. Everything he'd lived and survived by.

I think it's that depth of honesty in your plays that's so attractive. Beth and Teresa, in Tea in a China Cup, *for example, have got away from the traditions, the old style of life, if you like, but it's none the happier for that, it's a different kind of agony. It's the women who are always moving in your plays, the men seem to be stuck.*

In my experience, men, in general, are more entrenched politically and socially, whereas women, in general, seem to find it easier to cross boundaries and move on. Maybe that's because women are more practical and adaptable about real life *and* they have a better sense of humour!

In your plays there seems to be a strong sense of the male identity having been created by war and that identity endures in peacetime when the men seem redundant.

This is close to what male critics say, quite wrongly, about some of my plays. I write more about women than men, but the men in my plays have a role. I don't think that their identity has been 'created by war'.

Moving on to the term 'feminist' you and other woman writers, particularly in Northern Ireland, have always evaded that label and yet you suggest a feminist stance in The Belle of the Belfast City, My Name *and* Tea in a China Cup.

I'm very wary of labels in general and it's not particularly to do with feminism. I was brought up with a set of labels. I have been accused on the one hand of being a feminist and on the other of being sexist. As in my upbringing, the men in my plays are often offstage, but in more contemporary settings, such as *Joyriders* or *Clowns*, Arthur and Tommy are important characters. Critics never seem to comment when male writers depend on male characters and there are 'supporting' roles for women. That's our tradition, so it is not criticised.

I spent a lot of time at my grandmother's house on the same street as Graham Reid, the playwright, and we have completely different memories, probably because of gender.

The outsider is important in your plays.

There are two things here, the outsider as in *The Belle of the Belfast City* and the person who goes away and comes back. The outsider provides a commentary on what we are, a different gaze, and the response of the insider is also revealing. Again it relates to my own coming and going from England – seeing change which is so slow moving that it may not be obvious when you're part of it. Change is beginning to happen and I hope our work as writers has assisted.

A Bygone Culture

Like Marie Jones, Christina Reid commutes between geographic and religious boundaries, and her text *Did You Hear the One About the Irishman . . . ?*[1] combines Protestant and Catholic families in their welfare of respective prisoners in the Maze Prison (formerly Long Kesh). *Joyriders* presents the confusion of young Catholics who are merely government statistics in a Youth Training Programme. But Reid's informing culture is that of Protestant North and South Belfast, a culture more than a geographical location and forged and informed by history, by the Battle of the Somme and the annual celebration of the Battle of the Boyne.

The entrenched world of *Somewhere Over the Balcony* is endorsed within another culture, equally myopic and oppressive, and equally convinced of the supremacy of its own norms and traditions. While the men in West Belfast are absent because they are valiantly 'on the run' to save Ireland, the men of Reid's texts are absent because they have died in the wars, either the

Great War or the Second World War, in an effort to save Ulster. Women who have had to continue alone adopt patriarchal values in ruling clan and home. The few men who have survived are background uninfluential figures. Reid presents the irony of a society inhabited largely by women, but informed and led almost totally by masculine values and constructs.

Her first staged text, *Tea in a China Cup*, performed at the Lyric Theatre, Belfast, in November 1983, illustrates the exact boundaries and limited orbit of the society she investigates. As Sarah lies terminally ill she counts the days, not to her death but to the Twelfth. The walls around her are adorned with portrait photographs of generations of men in army uniform. The sustenance of the informing values, of the joint mythology and reality of war, is paralleled by the china tea set, an unused but much valued symbol of a brand of class and worth. When the auctioneer declares the set of china as more valuable than the portraits, Reid challenges the value of the literal inheritance of the unquestioned identity the portraits represent.

The limitations of a culture that demands so much personal endeavour and sacrifice for so little return are defined by constant juxtaposition of death and life, myth and reality. The coffin, 'the box', is a recurring image in Reid's texts. Bodies come home in boxes, and bodies leave the house and the street in boxes. In *Tea in a China Cup,* a fortune-teller predicts the arrival home of Sarah's husband in a box, and announces what Sarah already knows, that she is pregnant. The life of the child-to-be is already juxtaposed with death, and the closed locked worlds of the dead and the living become inseparable. This is a metaphor Reid employs often, and in her text *The King of the Castle*[2] the continuum of restricted and boxed-in lives becomes a central theme. Again, the image of the coffin is paramount and the play opens with the wake of Grandmother, attended by Great Aunt Cora, May and her eleven-year-old daughter, Eileen. Four generations of women are represented within a living room, not as portraits on walls but as female human beings, alive or, in the case of the grandmother, recently departed. The environment is completed by the street, with its mound of waste rubble from the Belfast Blitz, and the corner shop. The physical environment and its boundaries approximate the emotional and aspirational limitations of the inhabitants.

The title of the King of the Castle initially goes to Billy, who, of all the children clambering around the mound, has the best shop-bought kite. It is the envy of the others and, as always with Reid, a symbol, in this case of obvious flights of desire, which will never be realised. Great Aunt Cora has purchased a skipping rope for Eileen (last week's fad) and Eileen is able to exchange it for the coveted kite. The permanent fixture on the mound is Arthur, who has returned shell-shocked and demented from war. His pre-war personality and identity have been lost and he exists as some kind of appendage to society, relating neither to children nor to adults, scorned by both in different ways. Arthur's relationship with his previous normal existence emerges when May announces that both he and his dead friend, Stanley Porter, were her one-time 'sweethearts'. This is casually mentioned and difficult to integrate within the textual relationships, since she is married to an (offstage) man who refuses to appear if Great Aunt Cora is on the premises. May is expecting a baby, and given that daughter Eileen is eleven and there have been no intervening offspring, a textual gap appears.

The centrality of Arthur both to the children on the street and to the women in the house is disturbing and not exactly clarified. May makes him a kite because he longs for a real one so much. It is the laughing stock of Eileen and her pal Rose, who refuse to give it to him. In turn, Arthur captures a pigeon, ties it on a lead and invents this as *his* kite. The image is horrifying, the captured bird trying to fly on a noose. The children adopt this act as new mascot and 'fad', enshrining Arthur as King of the Castle. Their kite-flying becomes childish in the light of such acts of control and cruelty, and their childishness becomes metaphorical, entering a new phase of expression and 'play'. Warped values begin to mingle with the symbolic one of the mound itself, what it was – the pile of blitz rubble – and what it has become – a status symbol for small people growing up and learning the art of power and control.

Unlike the Tuckers of *Somewhere Over the Balcony*, Reid's men, if living, are referred to as drinking and betting husbands (by Rose in *The King of the Castle* and Sarah in *Tea in a China Cup*). According to Sarah, men 'have a weakness for the drink and the bettin'; she continues with the ironic comment, 'he was only a man, God help him'. The intuitive disregard for the existing male human being and the exaggerated respect for the dead war hero are always counterpointed and the awkward reality of the half-person returning from war is difficult to accommodate within fixed visions and concepts of heroism and masculinity. So Arthur in *The King of the Castle* becomes the central focus, defined as much by the reactions of others as by the tragedy he has suffered. The children chastise and spurn him. Great Aunt Cora decisively brands him as having had a dishonourable discharge, 'not able to fight like a real man', while May, representing an in-between generation, tries to mention the trials he may have endured and makes him the kite which becomes an object of scorn on the street. May's middle-of-the-road ineptitude is probably worse than the overt disgust of Great Aunt Cora. As Reid's depictions of three male generations of Sams (*Tea in a China Cup*) or Billys (*My Name, Shall I Tell You My Name ... ?*) represent political and social contiguity, in *The King of the Castle* the lives of women represent momentum and change, particularly in young Eileen's subconscious movement towards an understanding of Arthur.

Like memory in *Tea in a China Cup*, dream and fantasy operate in this text to depict young Eileen dancing with Arthur, repeated in the penultimate scene when they actually confront each other and Arthur experiences momentary lucidity in a flashback sequence to the death of Stanley at the Front. As the children kill the pigeon, Arthur visualises his friend's death and attempts to console Eileen, who is upset about the bird. Two different emotional scenarios merge and Cora and May, seeing only the literal, believe that Eileen has been molested. This joint response is challenged when Arthur says: 'You'll be wantin' Stanley's dog-tags, sir, he asked if they might be sent home to his sweetheart, sir.'[3]

Is Eileen the love child of Stanley and May? We certainly know that Cora has experienced similar circumstances in a previous war, when her sweetheart's medal was sent home to her. The innocent union of Arthur and Eileen suggests a deeper relationship and bond. The coincidences that Reid introduces, the litany of pain which cannot be expressed, particularly by Cora, and the implication of hidden secrets represent a society whose values were/ are submerged somewhere beneath truth. Like the carefully preserved, unused china cups and saucers in *Tea in a China Cup*, superficiality and tradition are more important to survival than encounters with truth.

While Rose, Eileen's pal, replaces Jean in the corner shop, her dreams realised, Eileen 'walks on' out of the street, out of its life and its boxed-in confines. Reid exposes a matriarchy that is as politically backward and conservative as any Irish patriarchy. She describes a poverty of spirit and imagination where occasional apparent gestures of generosity are not generous at all. The subtext presents a female collusion that inhibits truth or freedom. It does not matter whether Eileen is or is not Stanley and May's love child. It is enough that she could be. On the street that reality would be too hard to bear.

Reid's reality – that women collude in a general subjugation of humanity – is borne out in an early interview in 1984. Relating to *Tea in a China Cup*, she states:

> It's about women generally, and how they uphold traditions
> and beliefs which are positively harmful and damaging to
> themselves, because they've had it instilled in them that it's safer
> to do this, that this is what women should do, and no matter
> how unhappy women's lives are, they tend to re-create the
> same thing for their daughters; they're not truthful to their
> daughters.[4]

The generational acts of untruth by and among women are presented by Reid as universal and *The King of the Castle*, commissioned by the National Theatre, is not Belfast-based (although it is informed by that setting) and has been performed throughout the United Kingdom and further afield. The analogy of perpetuation of myth and bad faith which encumbers free thought relates back to broader truths within an Ulster context and is never far from the surface of Reid's analysis. The glorification of war and the sustained sanctification of its 'victims' or 'heroes' are challenged. The inevitability of suffering as part of a meaningful eternal plan is also constantly challenged. In the same way, a sense of roots and belonging within a dubious historical continuum can merge myth and reality to produce a fantasy world of the past and an untrue one of the present. The consequences for individual lives are enormous. Personal identity is lost to Beth in *Tea in a China Cup*, while Dolly in *The Belle of the Belfast City* may live in a fantasised world of golden memory, far removed from actuality. Similarly, the loyal men who have gone to war are purged of personal human failings in the romanticism and heroism of their deeds in battle, a perfect absolution. Within a broad social construct, interrogation of whatever hegemony is taboo.

We are reminded of the breaking of the silence, the coming to terms with the actuality of the Somme, as opposed to its mythical representation. Voicing the horror is difficult and painful but eventually life-enhancing, forward-looking. Sanctifying martyrdom devalues reality in a backward look that makes the past more important than the present or future. Reid summarises this in a reworking of a local ballad, preserving the final lines as ironic rather than sentimental commentary on all that is wrong with Belfast:

> It's to hell with the future and live on the past
> May the Lord in his mercy be kind to Belfast.[5]

The binary oppositions of women/men, peace/war, home/pub ensure that the two are kept well apart, textually and otherwise. This gendered segregation is as powerful as its religious counterpart. When a male *is* introduced, sectarianism, racism and sexism combine in masculine triumphalism.

In *The Belle of the Belfast City*, young Belle, daughter of Rose, who has emigrated to London, is of mixed race. Her presence as outsider, in more ways than one, becomes the device by which Reid may extrapolate the murkier depths of a staunchly loyalist Protestant psyche. Uncle Jack is a loyalist politician and described by Rose as 'a gangster, well connected with the Protestant paramilitaries, and other right-wing organisations in the UK'.[6] Innocent acts, like the smuggling of sausages from Dublin by Dolly during the war, become inextricably linked with gender. As well as the Fenian sausages, a statue of Our Lady has been purchased. Jack erupts to define the whole set-up as, 'Women! Women! Temptation! Deception! You're the instruments of the devil! The root of all evil.'[7] Women and Catholicism are equated. Jack's sexism is as embittered and deeply rooted as his sectarianism. His racism is equally imbued with religious connotations, mixed-race Belle described by him as 'the product of ungodly fornications'.[8] Violence, whether sectarian or racist, is articulated perfectly by Jack's sister: 'You love it, Jack. Violence is the woman you never had.'[9]

As in playwright Gary Mitchell's Protestant world, masculinity embraces sectarianism as a function of sexism, and, in Reid's case, racism also. She makes it more than clear that the only way out of a very sectarian, sexist historical morass is to *get* out. She configures change from outside, because it is impossible from within. Andrea in *My Name, Shall I Tell You My Name . . . ?* can interrogate the fixed values of the grandfather, whom she loves deeply, from afar in England. Similarly, Reid employs the innocent enquiring mind of young Belle on her first visit to Northern Ireland to highlight ingrained and almost subconscious prejudices which cannot be ratified by the outsider.

Constantly, women's lives in Reid's texts recall Edgerton's factual anecdote. Within this context, it is peculiar to read a response that accuses Reid of sexism. Referring to the absent men of her texts, *Theatre Ireland* states that the men 'are denied the right to appear in their own defence and dramatically as well as judicially, the play needs their presence. If they are the villains of the piece . . . we need to witness the tensions and collisions.'[10] The review goes on to say that Reid's writing is 'spasmodically marred by what seems to be a self-conscious effort to align itself with a sadly stereotypical feminist approach'. Reid's approach, however, is a search for a form that may define the lost lives of women who have worked to maintain the silence the men of the Somme and their official historians maintained and defended for more than half a century. It is a silence that women have perpetuated, possibly against their will, a form of collusion that could never be described as 'feminist', a form of life that denies any kind of freedom.

Reid's stage play *Clowns* (1996), a sequel to *Joyriders* (1986),[11] presents a contemporary society of twenty-something Catholics. The masculine identities forged by the Somme have been slotted into another kind of historical revisionism. The central icon in *Clowns* is a commissioned statue to commemorate the lives of female workers in Belfast's linen mills. Mother and child, surrounded by a rainbow of flowers, are the centrepiece of a very kitsch fountain. Textually, anomalies and representations are interrogated:

> TOMMY: It's an arty-farty fuckin' nonsense. When this was a mill, the women didn't work in freshwater fountains. They stood in water polluted with lead ... an' there were no friggin' flowers at their feet neither.
>
> ARTHUR: It's symbolic of human survival ... That's what the sculptor said at the unveilin'.[12]

The statue, like the portraits of *Tea in a China Cup*, symbolises a dubious continuum of romanticism which has been interrupted by contemporary events. In *Clowns*, woman is both victim and stoic survivor and the mill worker's statue becomes an increasing symbol of revised realities throughout the play. (It is the site of the onstage ghost of Maureen, whose tragic death is the finale of *Joyriders*.) Similarly, Reid underlines social change, if not progression, by creating the spanking brand-new shopping mall on the demolished site of an old mill that had been the premises of the Youth Training Programme of *Joyriders* in the 1980s. The teenagers of the earlier text become the adults of *Clowns* and trainee chef Arthur of *Joyriders* now owns The Harlequin Café-Bar, which becomes the setting of the play.

As the lives of young adults, trying desperately to 'get on', leave past histories behind, the speed and perhaps shallowness of contemporary life provide superficial substitutes for the no-hopers of *Joyriders*. The frenetic activity imaged by mobile phones, the constant opening of bottles of champagne, shopping at the high-street store Next, and the rapid comings and goings of Tommy, Johnnie, Arthur's wife, Iris, and the new baby (the fourth in six years) is paralleled by a series of manic offstage dramas. There is a rumpus about an out-of-date road-tax disc, during which Tommy lectures the Royal Ulster Constabulary on Marxism, Iris's car is stolen by joyriders, and a police inspector, driving a Jaguar, takes a pot shot at Johnnie for selling drugs to his teenage daughter. In addition, it is discovered that Iris is having an affair with the barrister next door. His daughter, Brenda, who baby-sits for Iris, presumably during the enactment of the affair with Brenda's father, purchases ecstasy pills from Johnnie for weekend consumption. So, on the eve of the 1994 ceasefires in Belfast, a distinct level of chaos reigns.

This textual freneticism is reminiscent of the depiction of an earlier time of socio-political upheaval – the beginning of the conflict in John Boyd's *The Flats*. As that play was criticised for lack of structure, the same mistaken criticism will be directed against *Clowns*. The structure here is subtextual, relating back and forward to the larger central issues – how do we come to terms with private and public grief and how do the living survive the dead? It is the theme of Frank McGuinness's *Carthaginians* and Reid confronts it in *Clowns* by placing the dead, if not centre stage, then central to the text. In the final scene of *Joyriders* the death of Maureen, and Sandra's rejection of Arthur are unresolved issues. In *Clowns* Reid returns Sandra from London eight years later to conduct an exorcism, like McGuinness's graveyard dwellers, to come to terms with that grief and to begin to live again.

In gender terms, the effects of the conflict are distinct. Males Arthur, Tommy and Johnnie manage to get through on a tide of activity and banter as Sandra struggles with the obsession of the loss of Maureen. It is Molly, Arthur's mother, who recognises and confronts the pain. To Sandra she says, 'you're mad with shock and grief and anger'. Ironically, it is Arthur who has physically suffered most and made a winning from it. As a teenager, he was shot by a plastic bullet and has a steel plate in his skull. The numerous jokes and references to the fact are counterpointed by a single issue of government compensation providing funding for his first business, which when burnt out by paramilitaries earned another round of government compensation, to facilitate the opening of the now-successful bistro in the new shopping mall. Arthur's misfortune, then, has turned to gold, while Johnnie, the hood who caused his sister Maureen's death, has promoted himself from joyriding to drug dealing. Tommy hangs on in between, running messages for both. The commercial gains of male pragmatism are in opposition to Sandra's psychological and emotional pain, her inability to function wholly. This is the centre of the play, as Sandra and Maureen's ghost, appearing and disappearing, share inner lives.

The ghost of Maureen is an almost perpetual presence on stage and transforms everyday banter to another level of meaning. All is not well with the world, despite new shops, state-of-the-art prams and expensive houses. The duality of Sandra's coexistence with Maureen must cease if life is to become liveable. Molly precipitates the exorcism by allowing Sandra to confront the reality of her imagination, to allow the imagined reality to ensue. Sandra begs Maureen to stop haunting her. It is Maureen who finishes the affair: 'I'm not haunting you, Sandra. You're haunting me.'[13] And so Sandra may return to London, alone and free of Maureen's ghost, which may reside in Arthur's well-meaning fountain back at the shopping mall. Sandra 'might just' return to Arthur in the not-too-distant future.

Here, Reid facilitates an imagining of futures and possibilities. Her subtext indicates that these do not occur overnight, following the announcement of ceasefires by male political leaders. The war in the heads is a much more complex and longer-term business, as imaged by Sandra's dual existence and its exorcism. The concept of real peace in Northern Ireland is feminine. The complexity of allegiance to the Crown and then to a state that threatens that very allegiance in the 1985 Anglo-Irish Agreement (backdrop to *The Belle of the Belfast City*) creates contradictions and complexities for a loyalist community. Reid presents a crumbling citadel whose masculine values can no longer hold. Even familial love is secondary to an essential liberation that does not exactly equate with happiness. The literal loneliness of Theresa, Beth, Andrea and Sandra is preferable to the stultifying communal acquiescence of their parents' generation. Reid's corpus of work creates an almost seamless cultural history of twentieth century Ulster, from the Somme to the Harlequin Café in Belfast's newest shopping centre. Within that history, her plays persistently interrogate the comfortable accepted norms and traditions of Protestant/Catholic, male/female. Andrea, *My Name, Shall I Tell You My Name . . .?*, Rose, *The Belle of the Belfast City*, Sandra, *Clowns* and Eileen, *The King of the Castle* all must emigrate to create new lives beyond the bygone culture of Belfast's socio-political heritage. An essential separatism is almost an analogy of another separatism, that of feminism in the 1970s. Reid's contemporary women who desperately seek some kind of inner and outer fusion, a healing, return to textually provide commentary on Northern Ireland. The strategy itself is a commentary on the lingering predicament of Northern Ireland and the failure not in addressing, but in implementing cultural change.

These same predicaments are central to Anne Devlin's analysis of a Catholic republican ethos, which thrives on the mythic and historic mix of fact and fiction so appealing to Reid's men and women.

5 Anne Devlin
The gap between ideology and behaviour

Interview with Anne Devlin, July 2002

You are known as a prose writer and screenwriter but it is the stage plays I want to talk about. You grew up in West Belfast as the daughter of a prominent political figure. Rolling two questions into one, your childhood memories and the influence of your late father's position in public life, how have these informed your writing and then what were your literary influences?

The important thing to note about Paddy's influence on me was that it came before he was a public figure. He went to parliament at the same time as I went to university. He brought me up to be a socialist. It was an emotional understanding. I had no intellectual grasp of what it meant at all. I always thought politics and literature and history were separate things. When my boyfriend, who was in the Young Socialists with me, introduced me to Raymond Williams, *Culture and Society*, then I realised the overlap. My copy still carries the date: September 1969.

It's very hard to explain what it felt like to be brought up by a working-class socialist in West Belfast through the 1950s and 1960s and to try to understand the intellectual basis of his beliefs – not mine, but his – in order to make them my own. Some of them I did make my own – I loved George Orwell, but because he attacked the Left so much, Paddy got angry. Orwell is interesting because he changes from being a writer who is writing from the memory of lived experience in *Wigan Pier* and *Homage to Catalonia* to being a greater writer who writes from the imagination in *Animal Farm* and *Nineteen Eighty-Four*. My father confirmed my decision to be a writer in a very clever way. In the 1960s when *Zee & Co.* had just been released as a film, I was looking at a double-page colour supplement photo of Edna O'Brien and Elizabeth Taylor. 'What a wonderful woman,' he remarks. 'Which one?' I ask. 'Edna O'Brien, of course. She's made a greater contribution to society.' I was being urged to find my model in the writer by my father, while my mother wanted me to be an actress and sent me to May Marrion's speech and drama classes. When I do a reading or write for the theatre, I reconcile my parents' tug of war.

Your plays did not open at the Lyric and the Royal Court's Ourselves Alone *only toured to Derry. What is the background to this?*

The title. The management at the Lyric Theatre were nervous about the title of my stage play. That was in 1985. When the Dublin Theatre Festival funded the Royal Court tour, it was performed in Limerick, Enniskillen and Derry, after Dublin. But Belfast said no. They were still nervous in 1994, so when *After Easter* opened at the RSC in May, they took that play instead.

Josie in Ourselves Alone *is a wonderful Irish archetype – the educated woman whose life depends on a relationship with a man. It seems to me that she could only have been created by a woman. How did you conceive and develop the character?*

I was in my thirties when I wrote Josie, so it's hardly surprising she's interested in men. It was after my divorce and before motherhood was to stun me for eighteen years. I'm glad to say she's still with me somewhere,

Josie. The best thing she says to Frieda is 'one day, when you come to the limits of what you can do by yourself ...' It took me years to integrate Josie's knowledge into my own life. Of course, it's my knowledge because I wrote the character, but I am not always aware of what I know until I write things: which is the whole point about creation, isn't it? But she's got an awful negative side, Josie – she hates the word fun! The only way I can distance myself from her position is to write comedy.

Ourselves Alone represents an indictment of republican politics, particularly in terms of gender – tell me more.

In writing *Ourselves Alone* I set out to test republicanism against feminism and feminism won.

In the new peace process where would you see Josie, Frieda and Donna?

That would take another play to explore, because I'm very time-specific as a writer.

Your new three sisters in After Easter *are reminiscent of the earlier trio. Did you intend even a tenuous link?*

Ourselves Alone was a tug of war between Freud and Jung. *After Easter* chose to explore Jung's side in the debate.

Did you consciously choose a more feminist form and stance in After Easter *following the naturalism of* Ourselves Alone.

I had to find some new voices – and I found Rose. The mother is missing from *Ourselves Alone*, just as the father is missing from *After Easter*. I'll have to write a play where both are present and in the same room and speaking to each other.

In After Easter *there is a strong sense of diversity in the finale, the power to create and free, as opposed to seduce and dominate, Michael's ashes in the Thames and the pastiche of 'On Westminster Bridge'. It spells out a vision and a political position – tell me more.*

I don't believe that creative power belongs anywhere but in the aesthetic. It's like Faust – Helen, the artist, speaks this line. Of course power in the aesthetic attracts the power in the institutions, so writers have to be courageous enough to defend their own integrity whether what threatens them is an ideology or a government or a relationship or any other powerfully armed group in society. You have to separate the citizen from the writer, because when the writer is creating, more is called up and the writer overcomes the beliefs of the citizen.

The old question: do you consider yourself a feminist?

This is precisely what I mean about the beliefs of the citizen. I am a feminist but when I'm writing more is called up.

Do you envisage more work based in Northern Ireland?

I am Northern and Irish. If I set a play on the moon, whatever I wrote would come out of that territory.

Ourselves Alone

Ourselves Alone,[1] an ironic use of the translation of 'Sinn Féin', charts the journeys of women who are struggling to comprehend and articulate their frustration, a first step towards liberation. The backdrop of lip service to women's rights is highlighted as no more than that. The text dramatises a basic hypocrisy in republican ideology. Catherine Shannon expresses the suspicion that tactical considerations are behind 'persuading a political leadership [Sinn Féin] to address women's issues. There is a huge gap between stated party policy on women's equality, and the views and actions of the party rank and file.'[2] In *Ourselves Alone* that gap is as much a female habitat as a male one. The women themselves unconsciously and necessarily collude in their own subjugation. It is the gap between ideology and behaviour that Devlin scrutinises.

   More stringently and transparently than any other Northern playwright, Devlin contextualises political conflict as a male construct in which women's lives are governed by orthodoxies that may be more conservative and authoritarian than those the male leadership strives to replace. Her work shows women in a variety of responses to a web of republican imagery and symbolism which defines their lives. Supposedly fixed realities are subverted and interrogated through plot, character analysis, and language and form, so that received traditions are juxtaposed against feminine alternatives.

Ourselves Alone portrays the lives of three young women in West Belfast during an eight-month period in the early 1980s and after the 1981 hunger strike.[3] Donna, the permanent resident of the domestic setting, is separated from husband and young son, and partners Liam, who is at the end of a five-year sentence and due for release from Long Kesh. They have a daughter, Catherine. Liam's sisters, Frieda and Josie, use the house to advantage. For Frieda, it is a drop-in centre which relieves the tedium of life with her maiden aunts, one of whom, Cora, has survived an explosion in which she has been severely damaged, physically and mentally (this has occurred during the 1950s IRA campaign). For Josie, the house provides convenient privacy for the conduct of a long-running clandestine affair with Provisional IRA leader Cathal O'Donnell, who is married and lives in the Irish Republic. The house is a 'safe house' for the Provisionals and Josie's excuse for living there is to assist Donna with child-rearing. She is actually in active service with the Provisionals, sleeping by day, on missions by night. Malachy is father of Frieda, Josie and Liam and local commander of the Provisional IRA.

Into this scenario arrives Joe Conran, an English freedom fighter for a variety of international campaigns and a graduate of Sandhurst, the British Royal Military Academy. He is a graduate of Trinity College Dublin and is married to a woman from the nationalist Bogside in Derry. His sister is married to a British Army colonel who is based at Sandhurst and has served in Northern Ireland. Conran has offered his services as political adviser to the Provisionals. Josie is nominated as his interrogator, has an affair with him and, at the end of the play, is pregnant with his child, as he is revealed as a British agent. Frieda has an affair of convenience with John McDermot, a Protestant 'sticky'.[4] She decides to leave Belfast to pursue a singing career in London. Brother Liam has been released during the textual timescale and, while back home with Donna, is conducting an affair with a barmaid at the local club, the official meeting place and social centre for the Provisionals. Danny is a musician and organises the entertainment at the club.

This simple plot outline itself reveals a series of frictions and contradictions between appearance and reality (Conran's and Liam's differing but significant duplicity), between motivation and its representation (Josie's domestic arrangements), and between nature and nurture (Conran's background and life).

The central theme of *Ourselves Alone*, the interrogation of exclusive and fixed ideology, is confronted in the first scene. Frieda is rehearsing a republican anthem, 'The Men Behind the Wire' – 'Armoured cars and tanks and guns/Came to take away our sons.' The establishment of a female voice within the lyrics is immediately undermined by a switch to male protest: 'Every man should stand beside/The men behind the wire.' The feminine passivity of onlooker and victim is contrasted with the exhortation to male action. The immediate encounter between Danny and Frieda, and then between Frieda and the two men who are stacking boxes in the club, establish the tenor and reverberations of the text as a whole.

> FRIEDA: Hey wee fella, what have you got in your box?
> FIRST MAN: Cotton wool balls.
> FRIEDA: I always thought there was something funny about you.
> FIRST MAN: See you wee girl, come the revolution, you'll be the first one up against the wall!
> FRIEDA: Well, I hope it's in the nicest possible way.[5]

Here, the juxtaposition of sexual innuendo by the female and unwitting sexual retort posed as political by the male very cleverly demonstrates a gendered linguistic supremacy.

Opposing forces again operate during Frieda's renewed attempt at the song. The 'fast and lively tempo', asserted by Frieda's rendering, is a response to the fact that Danny may allow her to perform her own composition some night, but not yet. Frieda's repertoire is a male prerogative. Perhaps more important is the resonance of Danny's response to Frieda's singing: 'You'll have to work hard against that tempo.' The fact is that women must 'work hard' against the inherent values of the particular culture they inhabit. Frieda must indeed 'work hard against' a 'tempo', and that tempo may be translated into the hegemony against which all the women must work hard, for survival and some level of independence. Contradictions rule in language and dialogue. Also, Frieda is literally becoming barricaded in by the boxes, the physical essentials of the republican struggle. She has no physical space, mirrored by the lack of emotional and psychological space she craves.[6] Devlin is forging the textual construct of the play, and defining difference.

Frieda is the only female within a male environment, a point she refers to later in the text.[7] Her presence among the male fraternity of the club is sanctioned by her ability to belt out republican propaganda, which is distasteful to her on two counts: because the lyrics eulogise men, and because their popularity precludes the possibility of ever promoting her own compositions. Ironically, her own lyrics for her song 'The Volunteer'[8] emulate the sentimental republicanism she so vocally despises. Capitulation to the dominant cannot guarantee the acceptability and stardom Frieda pursues. The subtext implies that, as local girl, she will be applauded for renderings of orthodox material, but never for her own creativity.

This first scene introduces all the elements of juxtaposition that govern the text. It ends with an innocent request by Frieda for sugar, as opposed to cotton wool balls. For the men, sugar is an essential ingredient of explosives; for the women, it is the basis of the recipe for home-made wine. Even the essentials of everyday subsistence have a gendered relevance. Devlin has introduced key elements which resurface later in the text. The supremacy of masculinity and its service by the female is established, as is its attempted but futile rejection by the female. Republicanism, internment and their related mythologies are exclusively male preserves, requiring the unquestioning support of women. In less than forty lines, and within a naturalistic framework, Devlin sets in motion a discourse of contradictions and opposites that inform the text as a whole. This introductory scene is among the most evocative and skilful in Ulster theatre.

Devlin authorises oppositional readings of republican mythology through the voice of Frieda. The hunger-strikers, whose images adorn the walls of the club, have replaced the icons of the 1970s, Pearse and Connolly, presenting a contemporary image of republican martyrdom and highlighting the seamless continuity of heroism from 1916[9] to 1981. Frieda's rejection of this concept when she says, 'We are the dying. Why are you mourning them,' is preceded by another reference to metaphorical death, addressed to her father:

> You know something, Father? You've been burying your
> friends since sixty-nine. But, do you know something else,
> your friends have been burying you![10]

Martyrs are portrayed by women as wife-beaters ('Bobby Sands beat his wife,' says Frieda), the living and the dead are burying each other in the muddle that lies between masculine ideology and female reality.[11]

The depiction of Aunt Cora as emblem of sacrificial heroism crowns this process of binary imagery. At the age of eighteen, as Cora was storing ammunition in her bedroom for young brother Malachy (now father of the girls Josie and Frieda), the token female auxiliary role again personified, the 'weeping' supply exploded and she was left 'blind and deaf and dumb and she has no hands'. In Frieda's words, 'they stick her out at the front of the parades ... to show the women of Ireland what their patriotic duty should be'.[12] Cora's condition enlists her sister and Frieda as carers, thus destined to spinsterhood. Three women are potentially relegated to lifelong conditions which have been instrumented by a single man and a communal patriarchal ideal. Cora's provision of imagery for the cause is converted by Frieda to its horrific reality. Silence, and especially female silence, seem to be a pre-condition of republicanism. Brendan McGurk describes Cora's silent condition as 'unspoken and unspeakable'[13] and 'symbol of his [Malachy's] control of the female, both linguistically and physically'. So too, Malachy's condemnation of Frieda[14] reinforces his predilection for female silence, even at the cost of death.

McGurk makes another important analogy, the objectification of the female body within 'male nationalist ideology'.[15] Having fulfilled its duty, the body, like the female psyche, is rendered functionless, redundant. One culture's heroine is another's victim. This representation of patriarchal ownership of the female body reaches its apex in the finale. Josie is pregnant by Conran, informer and double agent. In a twist of irony, Devlin portrays Malachy asserting his rights of blood ownership over the unborn child: 'This baby's my blood. If anyone harms a hair on its head ...!'[16] The image of protection coupled with violent threat is apposite, but finally Josie, like her aunts and Donna, is condemned to male custody. With the exception of Frieda, who will emigrate to England, the repression of an entire female family has been ensured by Malachy, the 'freedom fighter'. However, in an almost absurd scenario of chauvinism, it is brother Liam, representative of the new generation of freedom fighters, who tries to exert authority and owner-ship over the female body. He insists that Josie should have an abortion.[17] Not only is this assertive ownership an offence to feminism and the rights of women, contextually placed by Devlin, but an offence to the then prevailing republican policy on the issue of abortion.[18] Patriarchal values may shift to suit the occasion, and the final irony is that the conflicting views of father and son about sister and daughter's pregnancy both represent opposing but equally patriarchal domination of the female. Again, the female voice has been silenced, ignored. The concept of 'the women's right to choose' is heresy within this environment, where any and every choice is a male prerogative.

Male–Female Relationships

The dramatisation of the female characters and their relationships with men, whether sexual or as blood relatives, is a dramatisation of patriarchal oppression coupled with an element of female complicity. Both Donna and Josie represent Edgerton's informant's loneliness, Josie perhaps more per-sonally culpable because of her university education. She has been a foot soldier for the IRA, from building barricades in 1969 to transporting bombs ten years on.

Josie's political motivation is more personal and sexual than ideological – Cathal O'Donnell became role model and lover when he instructed her in the techniques of barricade building. Ironically, she was also learning the more metaphorical art of barricading her life. She waits for O'Donnell's un-announced appearances, and deludes herself with fantasies of a future, fan-tasies that are crushed by Frieda's information that O'Donnell has been in the North for some time, and has been flirting with her.[19] It would seem that Josie's ideology is a confusion of the sexual and political, a point which Devlin accentuates throughout in her portrayal of Josie's nurturing, which is far from feminist. Josie is prone to the private, and to personalising ambi-guities of the armed struggle. Her interrogation of Conran becomes an inter-rogation of her own personal commitment and internal motivation, as she outlines the facts of her background. In another of Devlin's reversals within the same scene, Josie's socialist principles are transcribed as materialistic jealousy.[20]

In Josie's personal interrogation of a republicanism that involved childhood trips to the annual Wolfe Tone commemoration ceremony at Bodenstown, County Kildare, without ever experiencing treats such as seeing the village shops, she expresses a bitterness that is personal and political. The credibility of her politics is interrogated by her willingness to accept the materials she envied as a teenager and which are now provided by Conran – perfume and weekends in Dublin hotels. Conran's duplicity is expert, professional and textually explicit. Josie's is more suspect and, as metaphor, perhaps more treasonous than Conran's. His professional act of treason is pitched against Josie's to herself.

A confused muddle of education, political indoctrination and cultural socialisation, all dependent on her need for sexual love, Josie is portrayed as a convenient and willing dupe of the apparently attractive elements of republicanism. Both O'Donnell and Conran exploit her thinly veneered vulnerability. Secrecy and the 'silence' McGurk refers to within another context are the fabric of her existence. The underground nature of her life, pledged to public silence and a private life of fantasy, is mirrored in her daily sleepwalking around Donna's house. Josie has willingly and officially enlisted for this half-conscious life. She is deeply unhappy and rushes from exploitation and rejection by O'Donnell to another version of it with Conran. The ease with which she may commute from one to the other, given her expressed pain at rejection by O'Donnell, is itself suspect. Here, as poignantly as in the brutal image of Cora, ambivalence and contradictions lead to tragic conclusions. Exactly like Cora's dutiful obedience, Josie's activism a generation later becomes the source of her victimisation, which will not be celebrated in parades, but will be paraded daily in community gossip and anecdote. Indeed, as Shannon suggests, her life, in the final exposition of plot, may be in danger.[21]

If Josie's life is one of half-conscious ideological confusion, Frieda's is one of fully conscious exploitation. She joins the Workers' Party in open rebellion against her father's politics and constraints on her life, and defies the communal politics of a community supporting the Provisional IRA. She does not conceal the fact that she is moving in with John McDermot for purely economic reasons. If Josie and Donna's subjugation is a cultural construct, Frieda's provides the other limitation on women's freedom, poverty. She distributes Workers' Party leaflets, which she has not read, and freely flaunts her self-interest. She is exhausted by her own identity, which has been forged by male family, her brother Liam and father Malachy. She is on the voyage out throughout the text and is the voice of retaliation and anger. Unlike Josie's educated but unconscious collusion, Frieda's single-minded offence to the dominant is based on a mixture of socialist principles and personal ambition, both of which she will strive to fulfil in essential exile. She cannot get far enough from West Belfast and even the move into McDermot's flat in the South Belfast university area provides another opportunity for intimidation, this time from Protestant neighbours.[22]

In comparison, Donna is the passive victim, accepting whatever deal life in West Belfast hands out to her. But there are complicated enigmas in her life and psyche and she is never what she seems. Freedom and bondage are fused within her life. She can live neither with nor without partner Liam and her interpretation of their relationship is always ambivalent, summarised by her own acknowledgement of some absurd satisfaction in the fact that since Liam is in prison, he won't get 'lifted' by the security forces. Ironically, he is safe in prison.[23] The implication is that Donna might be happier without dependence on a continuously absent partner, but the circumstances ensure the impossibility of such an ironic freedom. Her inability to secure independence is due to a process of socialisation that forced her initially into an unhappy marriage and then into a relationship that does not allow her the dubious privilege of the title 'prisoner's wife', but burdens her with all the protocol related to it.

Donna's acceptance of local orthodoxy makes her publicly invisible and a private psychological mess, addicted to tranquillisers and to debasement. Her house is as much subjected to exploitation as she is personally. The constant traffic in and out is not authorised by her. People arrive and are not to be questioned. Even simple domestic pleasures, such as hair dyeing, become larger issues. (If Donna arrives to visit Liam with dyed hair, he will, she jokes, think that she's 'running after someone'.[24]) Suspicion and jealousy exist inside and outside the prison boundaries, Liam controlling Donna, wherever he is. Similarly, as the women enjoy a glass of home-made wine panic ensues as Malachy arrives, leaving them money 'to buy chocolate', treating them as children on the one hand and responsible custodians of a safe house on the other. Reality and perceptions are in constant flux, emphasised by simple reversals. O'Donnell 'smiles' when his ulcer causes pain and Josie asserts that she is 'getting better at smiling at soldiers'.[25] Conran's response summarises the confusion, which is the outcome of constant contradictions throughout the text: 'if you smile to deceive, how will I know when it's for real?' – doubly ironic, given his own duplicity. No one can be sure of anything and Devlin juggles perception and reality to illustrate central contradictions between the real and the political, the patriarchy of colonialism and the more apparent patriarchy in the homes of West Belfast.

The Sociology of Violence as Represented by *Ourselves Alone*

Violence is never far from the centre of these lives. In *Ourselves Alone*, not a single act of violence is perpetrated by the security forces. Yet violence is a way of life, occurring with regularity within the confines of home and club. It is always a function of control and always perpetrated by men. This violence has been hidden for reasons relating directly to the conflict – the inability of victims to contact outside forces, anathema to their community, and the threat of further punishment should they attempt it. Terror within four walls might lead to public victimisation if declared.[26] The first study of domestic violence relating to the conflict was published by Eileen Evason in 1982, contemporaneous with the writing of *Ourselves Alone*. Evason quotes Cathy Harkin, a women's rights activist who stated that women had been living within an 'armed patriarchy'. Evason's evaluation of 'hidden violence' states that 'power gained outside the home may be deployed within it, adding an extra dimension to all the means which men normally have for oppressing women and engendering fear'.[27] A more recent report, post-ceasefires and post-Agreement, claims that 'many women living in the North are convinced that violence has not gone away – it has just moved indoors to the private domain of living rooms, kitchens and bedrooms'.[28]

It is impossible to assess whether the increase in reported instances of domestic violence since the ceasefires indicates an increase in violence, or an ability to report such abuse within a new environment that should free women from the offence of 'political disloyalty'. It is clear, however, that domestic violence has been endemic throughout the years of unrest. Angela Courtney of the Northern Ireland Women's Aid Federation echoes Devlin's depiction of quotidian domestic violence:

> The issues are the same: domination, power and control.
> Violence has become a way of life. There is an inability to
> negotiate and also an acceptance of violence as a way of solving
> problems. The underlying value base is the same – you can't
> have the brutalisation of society for 30 years without it causing a
> change in attitudes.[29]

The recurring incidents of violence in *Ourselves Alone* illustrate Courtney's assessment of violence as the sole means of problem-solving and an assertion of male domination and control over lives that might otherwise trespass the boundaries defined by men. An 'inability to negotiate' is pertinent in terms of *Ourselves Alone*, where there can be no sense of, or opportunity for, the kind of enlightened androgyny towards which, for example, McGuinness's characters are propelled in a voyage of discovery and liberation. There is no space, literal or metaphysical, for expression, thought or any kind of mutual understanding. Republicanism and its support base are unchallengeable dominants. Violence is the means by which male hegemony is maintained.

The textual incidents of violence are numerous: Liam's threatening of Donna at knife-point and his threat to Josie's unborn child; Malachy's attack on Frieda; and McDermot's threatening behaviour towards her. Furthermore, McDermot is attacked by Malachy's men. While these incidents are enacted, Devlin furnishes each with another layer of meaning which authenticates textual ambivalence. With the exception of McDermot's beating (for crossing political boundaries by entering the Provisionals' territory of the club), violence is domestic. Notably, McDermot is spared serious injury by Frieda's fabrication of the arrival of an army patrol, an ironic twist, with the legitimate forces of law and order (or the forces of imperialism) becoming guardians of female interests.

Violence is mostly related to knowledge of or suspicion of female transgression, political or sexual, either of which threatens male oligarchies.

Liam physically threatens Donna because her previous expedient marriage, long before her relationship with him, is somehow seen as a rejection of him. The fact that he was indulging in a series of affairs while training over the border at the time, and is currently enjoying an affair, evades his consciousness. Even from the confines of prison Liam's violent tendencies threaten, articulated appropriately by Frieda's linguistic combination of the vernacular and the metaphorical: 'When our Liam gets out of the Kesh, he'll probably kill both of us.'[30] But it is Liam's violent posturing over Josie's unborn child which is most male in its sense of ownership and Liam's belief in his triple authority as male, republican and brother. The ease of language with which Devlin expresses his righteousness implies not the author's but the cultural acceptability of such chauvinism:

> LIAM: Kill it. I want you to kill the child.
> JOSIE: But it's my baby – it doesn't matter about anything else.
> LIAM: It's his child.
> DONNA: No. It's not, Liam. It's what you never understood. A
>   child does not belong to anyone. It's itself.
> (*Liam grabs Josie's arms.*)
> LIAM: Do it. Don't force us.[31]

This act of domination crowns the series of others relating to violence. While Josie, Donna and even Malachy contradict Liam's assertions, the scene leaves the audience with the feeling that had it been physically within Liam's power to kill the child, he would have indeed done so.

Status and appearances become central. Devlin's cultural bastions of deceit and untruth are voiced by Donna, whose concern is that Josie may discover that the truth of her life with Liam is not what it seems:

> DONNA: Please, Liam. Please lower your voice. She'll think
>   you don't love me and then it'll be difficult for me to feel
>   good about myself and I'll have to leave here for shame and
>   I've nowhere else to go.[32]

Again, reality and the propensity for its denial are primary features. While Liam may threaten Donna physically, she is less concerned with the actuality than with others' perceptions of it. Longing for love mutates into a form of bondage which implicates the female in a collusion of possessiveness and insecurity, all dictated by the sovereign culture of patriarchy and its inherent and understated violence. Malachy can give his daughters money for chocolate in one scene, and beat them up in the next. Violence is not retributive, but a means of control, textually articulated by one of Malachy's henchmen: 'have you no control over your daughter?'[33] Even the politically sophisticated McDermot strikes Frieda when she suggests that flight from the republican ghetto has not provided her with inner liberation. Domestic violence is a norm, unremarkable because of that, but all the more insidious. Devlin portrays it as much an everyday feature of life in West Belfast as the pints drunk in its clubs.

Language and Form as Feminist Signifiers

Devlin's use of language and form is *her* controlling device. Amidst an apparent mayhem of fast-shifting, seemingly unrelated scenes, a formal strategy presides. The motion of the text flows as sporadically as the lives of the women themselves, who have so little control over their destinies or their everyday existence. Again, opposing forces of reality and fantasy, love and bondage, revolution and subjugation jostle for expression. Ideological tensions between the masculine construct of republicanism and its feminine opposition, the quest for personal and individual freedom, are matched by a linguistic tension between feminine and masculine.

Through the language of the women in their intimate moments of mutual soul-baring, Devlin creates oases within the text, displacing the dominant form of naturalism and its concomitant masculine language. As Anthony Roche has pointed out, 'There are only two occasions throughout on which all three women are together.'[34] But, on those occasions, while ideological difference is expressed, it is subverted by an ease of togetherness, a gendered communality that expresses itself through the domestic business of Act 1, Scene 2, and in discussion and sharing of their emotional and literal plights at the end of the play. Significantly here, they have all three lost partners, although Donna has taken on Danny as replacement for Liam; Danny makes her feel 'innocent',[35] presumably because, unlike Liam, he is untainted by republican activism. But it is in female dialogue or soliloquy that the poetic language of the feminine is most apparent, and the eloquence of inner lives highlights the basic meanness of the male dominance surrounding the women.

Donna, confused in love and life, transforms a superficial inadequacy into eloquent symbolism. Subjected to external forces and a psychopathic partner, she speaks with poetic authority and then, at the end of the play, with astute logic. Here, Devlin gives all the women space for individual finales of eloquence and meaning, in contrast to the stunted eruptions of Liam and the stage Irish sentimentality of Malachy. Donna's recurring nightmare vision is of the devil beside her in bed: 'He was lying with his head on my pillow this morning.'[36] The clear equation of Liam and the devil is reiterated at the end of the play when Liam must leave yet again, but like Donna's interpretation of the devil image, it (he) 'never goes away'. Donna's articulation of the dream sequence is also repeated in reality at the end of the play. In dream she says, 'I didn't have the strength to struggle any more.' Her finale is equally prescient and Chekhovian in its resignation:

> I think I may have lost the capacity for happiness . . . All my life
> I felt I had to run fast, seek, look, struggle for things and hold on
> to things or lose them . . . I felt for the first time the course of
> things, the inevitability. And I thought, no, I won't struggle
> any more, I shall just do. And all that time – longing – was
> wasted because life just turns things out as they are. Happiness,
> sadness, has really nothing to do with it.[37]

Devlin grants Donna a luxury of language that is lacking in her life, a reminder of possibilities unachieved but, certainly, given her innate intelligence, achievable. So, too, for Josie, love is a fantasy of language and image. As much as Frieda longs for liberation, Josie dreams of odd nights spent with O'Donnell. She translates the experience into fantasy, an exotic removal from the everyday: 'that bed is like a raft and that room is all the world to us'.[38] Josie deludes herself about the relationship because life has little else to offer in West Belfast until another outsider, Conran, comes along. He may be able to provide more realistic means of transport, but again Josie is as duped by him as she has been by O'Donnell. The raft image is pertinent. Temporary escapism leaves Josie with a lifetime's loneliness, a perpetual waiting and painful longing for the next appearance of an O'Donnell or a Conran.

Frieda's final speech, the finale of the play, summarises the distance between male and female. While the men may express solidarity only with literal images of martyrdom and rebellion (the hunger-strikers, the men behind the wire), the women are capable of a poetic imagery that unites them. Like so much of the text, this finale represents opposing forces, female freedom notably imaged by the moon and stars, and the intangibility of that freedom matched by 'catching phosphorescence' and an abstract sensual joy. This moment is interrupted by the literalness of men shouting, exerting a ludicrous ethical code on nude bathing:

> And we sank down into the calm water and tried to catch the
> phosphorescence on the surface of the waves . . . and the moon
> was reflected in the sea that night. It was as though we swam in
> the night sky and cupped the stars between our cool fingers.
> And then they saw us. First Liam and then John, and my father
> in a temper because we'd left our bathing suits on the beach.
> And the shouting and the slapping and the waves breaking
> over us.[39]

Female freedom and shared symbolic sensuality are framed by masculine ethics. But there is also an element of female complicity within the abandon, as the speech opens with Donna's declaration that she will marry 'Liam McCoy, one day'. Again, Devlin ensures that there are textual reverberations. In this case, Frieda's romantic and feminine evocation decries an earlier remark by Malachy that Frieda 'has a mouth like the QE2'.[40] The vulgarity of the analogy in the light of her ability for eloquence is apposite.

The suggestion of an alien political allegiance materialises at the end of the play, preceding the 'phosphorescence' speech, when Frieda expresses her desire for England as opposed to Ireland in literal terms of language: she will emigrate to England, because 'It's my language.'[41] Frieda's metaphorical asphyxiation by Ireland – 'I'd rather be lonely than suffocate' – is paralleled by Donna's literal attacks of asthma during Liam's periods of parole and accentuated on his release. Through a progression of images of death, the dead burying the living, the living death of individuals, 'we are the dying' – and Josie's willingness to 'die for an impossibility', Devlin presents a single cumulative image of collective social and cultural asphyxia. Odd momentary relief from the condition is expressed in a feminine language of intangible abstraction, rafts, phosphorescence, the catching of falling leaves. Significantly, of the three women, Josie, who has subverted her feminine self, has least participation in the discourse of feminine language.

Devlin's formal exposition matches the linguistic pattern. The frenetic hopping from one locale to another, and to different male–female pairings, reflects the undirected psychic unease of the women. The pattern shifts within a time frame of eight months, but the sense of linear time is not apparent, nor important to the text. The action shifts from the club, to Donna's house, to McDermot's house, to Josie and Conran in a Dublin hotel, to Frieda and McDermot in Belfast's Botanic Gardens, back to Donna's house, where British soldiers arrive to seek out Liam. The flux is accentuated by a preponderance of suitcases and people continuously on the move. There is no domestic or ideological base for most of the characters, except Donna, who has given up the struggle of life. Josie is constantly packing, while Frieda, according to McDermot, 'packs her case three times a week'.[42]

The finale, recalling an image of Scene 2 where the women are enjoying the female domesticity of hair dyeing and drinking home-made wine, unites the women in momentary private and emotional communion. The shouting of the men on the beach in Frieda's reminiscence is mirrored by the earlier and more literal intrusion by Malachy and Conran into Donna's home. Devlin implies through form that domestic privacy is as much an impossibility as emotional space. Coming full circle in feminine language, other more linear and masculine elements are recalled. Male intrusion on family members is as offensive as that by the British Army into Donna's house. Both intrusions are imperial. The family intrusions frame the text, with the army's intrusive surveillance occurring midway, one reverberating on the other. So, too, the pleasure and relative happiness of the community of women, as depicted by the second and final scenes, is interrupted throughout the text by short expositions of male–female discourse. As Devlin emphasises through the voice of Donna, 'We're all waiting on men.'[43] She then demonstrates the outcome of that 'waiting' in a series of encounters between the pairings.

The oddest of these encounters occurs in Act 2, Scene 4, between Frieda and McDermot in Botanic Gardens. The setting, outdoors and out of West

Belfast, is as textually dislocated as the occasion is thematically bizarre. Cynical Frieda and politically astute McDermot are deliriously catching the falling leaves of autumn – 'for every one you catch you have one happy day next year'.[44] Significantly, Frieda's romp with nature is framed by male intrusions, which are, in Devlin's arrangement, more symbolic than literal within a scene that is itself textually symbolic. While Frieda is counting leaves, McDermot is busy counting the Workers' Party's latest vote in North Belfast.[45] The masculine–feminine opposition is distinctly clear. Frieda announces that a man has been following her: 'he was blocking the only way out'. This analogy to her relationship with McDermot is suitably derided by him, and as easily as he colludes with the police who have been called by residents complaining that the pair have been 'causing a disturb-ance', McDermot colludes in an act of treachery against Frieda, less obviously brutal than Liam's against Donna, or Conran's against Josie, but dismissive in its insinuation of Frieda's state of mind: 'She was depressed, so I took her out to catch leaves.'[46] Innocent pleasures, whether catching leaves or phosphor-escence, are negated by male intrusion. Finally, as Frieda's path has been obstructed by a man following her, *she* is accused by the police of 'causing an obstruction'. Hence, Devlin's overall formal strategy is telescoped into a single scene – the innocence of any free female activity obstructed and pro-nounced aberrant, whether it be hair dyeing, catching falling leaves, drinking wine or nude bathing. A male conspiracy of police, army and republicans rules every waking and abstract moment.

Two formal techniques operate alongside each other, the linear develop-ment of plot, of male–female relationships and their negative outcomes, and the feminine circularity described above. This is an unusual achievement, a text that is both masculine and feminine, but not feminist, although dealing with feminist issues. Neither does it present the androgyny, the union of gendered opposites, which defines other texts. There is no internalised com-bination of, or meeting between, the opposing forces of gender in form or language. A separatism is skilfully enforced to underline 'the gap' between patriarchy and its challenge by women. The dominant mode of naturalism is interspersed with moments of *écriture féminine*, always highlighting a submerged potential. But a potential is all that it is, stifled and asphyxiated by patriarchy. Devlin triumphantly employs and controls the masculine dominant form in order to subvert it.

Roche, in discussing the Chekhovian 'decentring of emphasis, politicised by Brecht and taken on by women's theatre as a precondition of performance style and often of creation through collaboration',[47] finds difficulty in the non-feminist stance of Josie in her interrogation of Conran. He also finds the male–female hierarchical juxtaposition, as personified by Josie, problematic: 'Josie's position has no place within this feminist environment.' In response, two things can be said. First, Roche fails to grasp that Josie has moved closer to becoming surrogate male and, as such, she denies her femininity within the overriding silence imposed on her. She is symbol and outcome of the hegemony that Devlin outlines. Josie is willing victim and dupe. Second, the fact that there *is no* 'feminist environment' in Devlin's play eludes not only Roche but most other critics as well. Indeed, the 'hierarchical' posturing of Josie's interrogation is usurped by the male hierarchy of O'Donnell and Malachy, who have been secretly monitoring the proceedings. Josies's apotheosis within the republican movement is subverted, again by males who do not and would not allow her such autonomy or authority. And, ironically, she is personally held accountable for Conran's treason, while the men abdicate responsibility. She herself is unaware of their surveillance – the watched watching the watched. Far from creating a feminist text or a feminist environment, Devlin is at pains to show that in the world of *Ourselves Alone* both are impossibilities – ultimately, that is what her text is about.

Devlin's subtext indicates, repeatedly and clearly, that a feminist text cannot be created from an examination of the culture and controls of sexist determinism which govern the lives of women. A thematic and feminist exposé does not necessarily constitute a feminist text. Roche's analysis is as male as that of Devlin's own males, and ignores the binary approach throughout the text. His disappointment is a consequence of Devlin's talent for fissure and disruption, which defies mainstream and even feminist structures and analysis. When the text contradicts Roche's analysis, he fails to see that these very contradictions are central to theme and exposition.

Helen Lojek, comparing the function of the outsider in McGuinness's *Observe the Sons of Ulster Marching Towards the Somme* and Devlin's *Ourselves Alone*, also criticises the gendered dichotomy within which 'men are out;

women are in'.[48] I challenge the assumption that 'women are in' – they simply represent a possibility for difference, socially, morally and politically, within the closed and ghettoised realities of Devlin's environment. As Greta asks in *After Easter*, 'Why does everything have to be so literal?'[49] *Ourselves Alone* relates with integrity to the facts of the environment of Northern Ireland. To comply with post-feminist theory would deny the truth of factual evidence. Lojek cites Jill Dolan's general thesis in reference to *Ourselves Alone*: the strategy is 'not to abolish gender categories, but to change the established gender hierarchies by substituting female values as superior'.[50] Devlin highlights gendered inequity as it affects a particular community which is in the process of waging war on the inequities of imperialism. It is this very irony that becomes Devlin's theme. Inclusion and some balance between opposites are impossible illusions within the environment she creates. To criticise her for expressing a dichotomy, and the impossibility of pluralism or revisionism, is to miss the point of the text. The 'feminine' is disregarded and insulted culturally to the extent that a feminist text is impossible.

Julia Pascal criticises the fact that in *Ourselves Alone* 'women's lives are lived through men'.[51] Pascal sees an offence to feminist sensibilities, in the same way as Roche sees an offence to feminist form. Both responses emanate from a determinism that obscures relativity. For Pascal, the realities of the lives of women in West Belfast during the early 1980s cannot be understood in terms of European post-feminism. She assumes that European feminist values are a shared global culture, reaching as far as West Belfast. Edgerton's knowledgeable depiction of a 'feminist backwater'[52] is more accurate. Similarly, Roche would prefer to see Devlin apply values of feminist criticism and form. Devlin is writing from a feminist consciousness, but about an environment and society that precludes such a luxury.

Historical Evidence

The veracity of the status and role of women in Northern Ireland during the 1980s as depicted in *Ourselves Alone* has been authenticated by academics such as Shannon, who found that the lives of women during the conflict went unnoticed and undocumented until that decade. She recognises the ideological and oppositional debates within Devlin's text as reflecting those of the period, and waged also 'between revisionist and anti-revisionist historians'. Shannon states that 'the play does indeed personalise and render concrete the atmosphere of the time'.[53] She also posits, however, that Devlin presents stereotypical republican women who are not fully representative. But the view that republican compatibility with feminism is problematic (at that time) must be accepted. In Shannon's reading, Devlin was not 'unique' in her assessment that 'the ideology, structure and tactics of contemporary republicanism were inimical to the best interests of women'.[54]

Republicanism has not admitted that its struggle was not against all forms of oppression and may, in fact, have endorsed the repression of women. Simple political equations which may operate within a European context and indicate a union of feminism and left-wing ideologies do not occur in Northern Ireland, and the relativity of feminism may be misunderstood, particularly by critics outside the confines of Devlin's environment.[55] Those who find the landscape of Ourselves Alone deficient in feminist terminology and exposition inhabit a system of cultural politics that rarely applies to Northern Ireland. The idea that the 'war' has bred and instilled a feminist self-determination, the willed belief of some, is undermined by Devlin's evidence. Comfortable assumptions that 'a Republican feminist agenda presents a tangible and powerful vision of a future Ireland which brings equality to all its citizens'[56] are refuted. This statement, from a London-based feminist journal, is qualified by the remark that 'Sinn Fein is still a male-dominated party, and as such cannot always be trusted to make women's interests a priority'.[57]

Devlin's truth lies in the voice of Frieda, whose life and identity have been forged by her family, and particularly by brother Liam. As she says, she has never had the opportunity to be herself. Identity is preordained by male misdemeanour:

> When did I ever have a chance to be myself? My father was
> interned before I was born. My brother's in the Kesh for bank
> robbery. You mention the name McCoy in this
> neighbourhood, people start walking away from you
> backwards . . . Nobody knows you. Nobody knows you exist.[58]

When Frieda adopts the spurious political mobility of Liam, she is treated as an outcast. While Liam may be a Provo one day, a sticky the next, a member of the INLA, or a member of Sinn Féin, Frieda is ostracised by him for her tentative links with one of his old causes. For women, political agendas become gendered. They all unconsciously adopt Donna's approach. For Donna, life is a waiting game.[59] There is no luxury of ideology for these women, and certainly no possibility of empowerment within a regime that cannot even begin to recognise that women deserve a life and independence of their own. Historian Joseph Lee's statement that Irish people have a 'capacity for self-deception on a heroic scale'[60] is easily transferable to Devlin's portrayal of Northern republicanism in the 1980s.

The mode and discourse of *Ourselves Alone* is heightened and exaggerated in *After Easter*. The two texts are companion pieces, with the latter realising an ideal of personal fulfilment that is remote and intangible within the relative cultural confines of the former. Life lived beyond the territorial boundaries of Northern Ireland – Frieda's dream in *Ourselves Alone* – is Greta's reality in *After Easter*.

After Easter

Conventional plot analysis is not applicable to this text, which deploys characters within a range of situations and relationships whose symbolism is more important than narrative and inner journeys more relevant than the linear story of what happens. The female trio of *Ourselves Alone* is replicated by three blood sisters who, in their mid- to late thirties, are older than the women in the earlier play. Greta is married, has eleven-year-old twins and a new baby and lives in Oxford. Aoife, a teacher, has five children and lives in Northern Ireland near Toomebridge with her husband. The youngest sister, Helen, is unmarried, works as a commercial artist and lives in London. Their mother, Rose, runs a small drapery business from the front of the family house on the Falls Road. Michael, the father, is from a rural background and Aoife lives in his old family home. The family is completed by Manus, who is twenty-four and lives at home with his parents.

Greta has had a nervous breakdown and has been institutionalised. On release, she is taken by Aoife to Helen, who lives in a modern apartment and has the lifestyle of a London career woman. The trio leaves for Belfast when they hear that their father has suffered a heart attack. Greta visits an aunt, who is a nun, and steals a chalice and communion wafers to distribute to the people of central Belfast; Helen's hired car is vandalised in the grounds of the Royal Victoria Hospital; and brother Manus is harassed by the British Army as he delivers First Communion veils for his mother. Michael dies and during the wake there is a disturbance outside the home, in the course of which the family seeks shelter under a table. The finale occurs one week later on Westminster Bridge, where Greta and Helen try to manage a drunken dispersal of their father's ashes into the Thames. The narrative, as such, provides an excuse for metaphysical exposition, which is just barely related to textual incidents. The dominant naturalism of *Ourselves Alone* is replaced by an internalised focus on psychic development.

As the title implies, the text deals with personal resurrections, tinged, as always in Devlin's work, with irony and levels of meaning. The hegemonies of religion and nationalism, replacing that of republicanism in *Ourselves Alone*, are interrogated by the communist politics of the father, and exorcised by Greta to attain her 'resurrection'. Nationalism is portrayed as a construct of defeated idealism, and religion as an autocracy that manifests itself in Greta's madness, although this psychotic possession may be more related to community economics than spiritual well-being. Both religion and nationalism create communal subservience and private mayhem – the central theme of the text. Absolutes are challenged to reinstate Greta's personal equilibrium, and a harmony, or tension, of competing values finally represents the freedom that cannot be achieved by literal escape. Devlin combines character, form and language to reconstruct Greta's sense of identity and through that to present her own world vision.

Character and Identity

If gendered contradictions between male hierarchies and female dispossession pervade *Ourselves Alone*, ambivalence and contradictions define the character of Greta in *After Easter*. The other characters become the symbolic props of her psychic excursion, challenging or reinforcing her depositions on life. Patriarchal control is replaced not exactly by matriarchy but by cultural definitions which can be either endorsed or challenged. The lives of the sisters are not gauged against or defined by male authority. A more subtle form of social conditioning is involved.

All three sisters live very different but equally schizophrenic existences, none of them happy. Greta's fractured psyche relates to her inability to fulfil her artistic ambitions, to live in an English culture, and to come to terms with her upbringing and, in particular, a religious education which was contested by her father's communism. This is paralleled by Helen's manufactured identity. She talks with an American accent because, for social and political reasons, she does not wish to be identified as Northern Irish in London. Aoife, on the other hand, is obsessed with Irishness, almost to a degree of racism, and defines her identity by nationality. Even astronomy offers an absurd nationalist relevance for Aoife, who misidentifies the Pleiades as the Plough – 'the symbol of the Irish Citizen Army'.

Helen and Aoife represent opposite extremes of nationalist consciousness, while Greta floats helplessly around the issue, unable to find comfort or compromise. The introductory scene between Greta and psychiatrist Campbell establishes Greta's discomfort with her Irish identity in England and her unwillingness to remedy this by mixing with other expatriates:

> CAMPBELL: Why don't you meet with some other Irish people?
> GRETA: I don't know any, I live in Oxford . . . Anyway, it seems a bit vulgar, you know, to go out looking for people who have the same or a similar accent. Oh I know it's something you English do all the time, but frankly that's a good reason for not doing it.[61]

Miserable within one cultural context, Greta is unwilling to try another. This literal explanation has metaphorical relevance, the opposites never achieving synthesis. Greta cannot live contentedly either in England or in Northern Ireland and she plays one off against the other. Aoife explicitly reinforces the concept within the confines of her nationalist perspective – 'the English and the Irish cannot love each other'.[62]

Polarity of nationhood is matched by a religious segregation that is expressed through Greta's psychotic obsession and its comparison with the vocational religion of her Aunt Eilish, who is prioress of a convent in Belfast. Greta has no institutional links with Catholicism and has not brought her children up as Catholic. Yet her hallucinations are religious. On Pentecost Sunday, seven weeks after Easter, she witnesses tongues of fire.[63] On the feast of the Purification, she accidentally sets her hair on fire while lighting candles for a dinner party. On her birthday she has seen the devil, 'dressed like an old priest'. Greta's hallucinations are a source of envy for Eilish, who describes the psychosis as 'a state of grace' – one person's madness is another's dream of sanctity. Eilish urges Greta to seek the protection of a religious order, and to begin by taking communion. Greta literalises the advice by stealing the chalice from the local monastery and distributing wafers to people in a bus queue.

This secularisation of religion, as symbolised through reversal, is repeated by the imagery of the Trinity. Greta believes that she is the Holy Ghost. Helen, chief organiser and surrogate male, could be seen as God the Father, with Aoife as Son. It is not so much the gender reversal that is important as the secularisation of religious mythology. Aoife dutifully attends Sunday mass; Helen, of course, does not. At one moment Greta becomes a nun, and at the next steals the chalice from the church.

The trio displays the same pattern in their relations with men. Helen is almost surrogate male in her emotional detachment. She has affairs only with rich married men, whose marital status secures her independence. She is ruthlessly matter of fact about her male behaviour: 'I don't have visions; I have sex.'[64] In an unusually confessional moment she reveals that she would like to have a relationship with a particular man, but the complications are too enormous and life is easier without such commitment. Helen skilfully avoids Aoife's curiosity and instead of showing any evidence of love, asserts her usual control:

> AOIFE: Is he important to you?
> HELEN: If I went away he would fall apart.
> GRETA: Are you likely to go away?
> HELEN: Yes, he lives with someone else.[65]

Devlin here combines disparate elements within a few lines. First, it is the male who is proffered as victim, while the female is in charge, and second, the linguistic use of 'went away', 'go away', suggests more than simply leaving a relationship. It is a physical separation into a different territory. Helen's objective is self-preservation at whatever cost, denying the possibility of love in order to avoid pain and loss. In every sense, this is the antithesis of the movement within *Ourselves Alone*, where the women become literally and metaphorically 'barricaded in'.

While control is asserted and the business of life is superbly managed by Helen, there is little sign of inner happiness. At the other end of the spectrum is the quotidian boredom of attachment, which is Aoife's lot. She brightens the conventionality of her life in Toomebridge with fantasies of affairs. She uses the flowers sent by Greta as a tease to her husband and a sort of relief mechanism for her own tedium. The pretence that the flowers are from a lover who 'was going to arrive and take me away'[66] is dispelled by a phone call from her mother, the voice of reality and convention. Aoife envies Helen's life, but is utterly incapable of replicating it. She would like to borrow a little of Helen's style by converting the barn in Toomebridge into an inner-city-type apartment: 'she has a great flat – I mean, she lives in a white loft with maple floors and blue drain pipes. I can't wait to get home and do our barn up.'[67]

For Greta, sexual relations are not a major preoccupation. She does not fantasise about affairs, like Aoife, or even wish to regain the passion of husband George, who is himself having an affair. This element of her life is, like others, adrift. Her description of the loss of her husband's love is pragmatic and remote, as detached as Helen's. Greta relates to Eilish the conflicting identities with which her husband has to cope: 'He was a Marxist historian. He thought he'd found a radical secular emancipated woman, and instead he'd got a Catholic mystic.' Significantly, she describes compartmentalisation, that she shut off her grief 'in another room and, lived in the outer room of ... life'.[68] Again, the causes of Greta's dysfunction are related to segregation and an inability to combine emotions and experience. But the remarkable quality in the play is Devlin's generosity to male characters.

Unlike *Ourselves Alone*, this text does not blame or accuse. Personal responsibility is not a gendered issue and, through Greta's journey, we see its necessary acceptance by an individual, free from the monoliths of the earlier play.

Lives are no longer led through relationships with men and the women are not dominated by them. Men are marginal, textually and subtextually. In their varying ways, the three women break with the traditional values espoused by the male hierarchy of *Ourselves Alone* and the culture of auxiliary support within which women in Northern Ireland have had to exist. Devlin achieves this by exiling Greta and Helen to England, where they must confront issues larger than the war in West Belfast. Within a broader cultural spectrum, they must broaden their own outlooks and accept responsibility for the conduct of their lives. In order to do so effectively, inner journeys must parallel those of the literal escape across the Irish Sea.

The character of the mother is a rich mix of similarity to and difference from her daughters. Rose displays no intellectual or emotional enlightenment. Nationalism, for her, is an operational function, not an ideology, a condition of rioting, surveillance and daily nuisance. Religion is the arbiter of whether or not she will be granted a school-uniform franchise to augment her trade in First Communion and christening outfits. The abstractions of nationality and religion, which so deeply torture Greta, are for Rose pragmatic instruments of the economy of her small business. When Greta's city-centre expedition with the chalice comes to light, Rose's response is unrelated to any concern about her daughter's mental health or the effect of the incident on Greta's chances of gaining custody of her children: 'I might as well close the shop. Are you trying to put me out of business?' Rose is as capitalist as her husband is communist. While inhabiting different worlds, Rose's self-centred interest in making money resembles Helen's detachment. Ironically, Helen, the business woman, describes her mother as having 'cash registers for eyes'.[69] (Significantly, it emerges that while Rose sends clothes to Eilish's orphanage, Helen has been secretly sending money.) Rose is closest to Aoife. Culturally, they share the same space, but Rose's personal limitations do not allow her to acknowledge the wider limitations that frustrate Aoife. Greta's condition, it is suggested, may be partly a reaction to Rose's violence and withholding of maternal love.[70]

While Rose's lack of nurture has shaped her daughters in different ways, Devlin exploits the features to ironic effect. Rose is comfortably socialised within the very constructs her daughters struggle to interpret and defy. Characters become symbolic beyond their minimal narrative functions, and opposition is not between male and female but within a female matriarchy. Male appearances provide another means of presenting opposites. Manus is gay, and Paul Watterson, who deals with Helen's car vandalism in the grounds of the Royal Victoria Hospital, is a Catholic policeman. Michael's resurrection from the coffin is a Joycean joke on Devlin's part. She exploits Greta's hallucination to emphasise the textual theme through the words of Michael: 'Everything equals everything else. I don't believe in hierarchies.'[71]

Madness, Language and Form

The function of feminine 'madness' has been addressed by feminist critics, mostly in relation to nineteenth-century literature, and particularly to the text of Charlotte Brontë's *Jane Eyre*. It is no accident that Devlin chooses the mode for her contemporary analysis of a society adrift from its own stated norms of democracy and pluralism. Madness, as personified in Greta, is the classic madness, analysed by feminist critics and related closely to their inter-pretations of psychoanlaytic treatments.[72] Greta's asphyxiation or oppression is related to her early family life and lack of love from her mother. Her innate disruptiveness has been silenced for so long that it erupts in antisocial behav-iour — storming out of dinner parties, sitting down in front of buses and distributing communion wafers to shoppers.

Greta's sit-down, her overwhelming revulsion to the patterns of roses on wallpaper reminding her of her mother, Rose, and her religious visions, all represent what Juliet Mitchell defines as the symptoms of the female psychotic, 'rejecting present reality and replacing it with a delusion that contains a grain of truth from some reaction to a past event'.[73] Greta's marriage to a Marxist historian also replicates what Phyllis Chesler refers to as 'the incest taboo, the preference for "daddy", followed by falling in love and/or marrying powerful father figures',[74] a symptom of floundering identity within patriarchical society.

Devlin gives madness a voice, which has not been the privilege of nineteenth-century counterparts, and presents Greta's predicament as a func-tion of patriarchy. Devlin's portrayal, revealing her theoretical knowledge of feminist criticism, places her alongside Frank McGuinness. It is perhaps not entirely accidental that the two women who suffer most, psychologically, from patriarchy, and who endeavour most to overcome sexism and misogyny, share the name Greta, as well as an ideology. (McGuinness's Greta in *Carthaginians* is similar to Devlin's Greta in background and renunciation of it, although McGuinness's Greta is not so openly dysfunctional.)

The espousal of a feminist critique of psychoanalysis, as portrayed by Devlin's Greta, is matched by a consistently feminine language and a formal shape that defies linearity. If feminine language, to take a single example, may be defined as 'open, nonlinear, unfinished, fluid, exploded, fragmented, polysemic, attempting to speak the body, i.e. the unconscious, involving silence, incorporating the simultaneity of life as opposed to or clearly different from pre-conceived, oriented, masterly or "didactic" languages',[75] then Greta's language consistently matches that long roll-call. First, verbalisation of the unconscious is her norm throughout, relating visions, talking to the dead and constantly reliving abstracted interpretations of the past. Simultaneously, silence is Greta's secret weapon, one which she endorses strategically in the introductory scene, where everyone else's screaming ensures that she is 'very quiet'.[76] Greta may also move from silence to announce that she 'is breaking the rules',[77] defying hierarchies and asserting her right of articulation, as opposed to silence. The concept of 'breaking the rules' becomes linguistically important, as Greta opposes that hegemony of silence which is so deeply engrained within her psyche. She breaks the rules, and the family is unable to assimilate the consequences, literal in the offence against the Catholic church, and metaphorical in terms of Greta's journey.

In the text opposing forces operate, not in a mode of tension but of strict irrational contradiction. Student sit-down protests of the 1970s, repeated by an individual in the 1980s, transform into personal suicide attempts. The difference between politics and madness is a matter of numbers. The safe environs of a hospital become the playing fields of thugs and joyriders. Rose not only knits, but drags Aoife into collusion, by constructing a fisherman's jumper that will never be worn by husband Michael. Linguistic and formal oppositions eventually become the property of the family members, who wear first communion veils as the soldiers invade their backyard, and, in very mundane textual reality, surpass themselves in an evocation of imagery that would seem to be more Greta's preserve:

> HELEN: There's a carpet of snow in the front seats.
> AOIFE: It's snowing?
> HELEN: No. It's raining broken glass.

Of course, the 'broken glass' is literal, accentuated by Aoife's response, but there is the beginning of a transferral of Greta's language to the sisters, lessening the emphasis of Greta's dysfunction and inability to harmonise. Devlin unites different modes of language in an almost imperceptible blend, where there is little distinction between Greta's feminine language and the eventual discourse of the other sisters. This movement is marked most formally when towards the finale the family is united under a table because of disturbance outside. Greta becomes more literal than the others and actually exerts some authority. As mother Rose is accused of a series of personal wrongdoings by son Manus, it is Greta who intervenes. Within this exposition of Manus's declaration of homosexuality and another literal confrontation regarding Helen wearing the sacrosanct jumper which has been knitted for Michael, Greta stands up for the mother, who has perhaps been one of the causes of her psychosis. This generosity of spirit from Greta marks a departure, a new beginning. It may leave the other members of the family with more to think about. It is when the fissures between the supposedly 'normal' family members erupt that Greta comes into her own territory, one from which she has been lost and adrift for a very long time. Through language, the ambivalence between reality and imagination is underlined:

> GRETA: I was dreaming . . . it was raining.
> HELEN: It is raining. Look. What does that mean – when the
> outside and the inside are the same, I wonder?[78]

Here, Helen is stating Greta's position. Greta has reached a state of awareness and contiguity where, for the first time, internal and exterior worlds operate in some kind of harmony. This is finally expressed in the fusion of imagery of the final scene, where Greta may express joy and exhilaration in a coalescence that is both intellectual, personal and literary. She may recite 'On Westminster Bridge' and easily juxtapose it comically with the literal present. It is a scene that takes the characters away from West Belfast, and allows them to celebrate a victory over past lives, a liberation that is also a kind of exorcism of their father in distributing his ashes, and one that allows Greta to quote literature, and to absorb it through meaningful contemporary references:

> Earth has not anyhing to show more fair – than the new
> MI6 building over there.
> Dull would he be of soul who could pass by a sight so
> touching – as the homeless on Westminster Bridge.[79]

Here, past and present, reality and literature, and old and new lives are combined. In comparison it is eventually Helen, who has harboured and ignored opposites, who must also, as well as Greta, face her life. Her expression of these feelings and their relativity to her external and internal world are articulated:

> The worst thing I did was to squander a great gift. I took my
> gift, which was very powerful, and I used that power to seduce
> and dominate. When I should have used that power to create ,
> and free.[80]

Devlin here realigns the supposed madness of Greta with the very assimilated world of Helen into a picture that combines varying world-views and opposites into a unity. In a beautiful movement of formal achievement, Devlin shifts the emphasis from one sister onto another and, in so doing, shifts the textual emphasis onto another level, formally embracing all characters in a future, whether abstract or lived. When Helen states, 'It's my memory that stops me from seeing. I'm concentrating on forgetting', Greta becomes formally liberated.

After Easter's finale shows Greta at the end of her journey and rehabilitated with her baby, narrating a story in which all the imagery of the preceding text comes into play, but in a mood of acceptance and quiet calm: 'I could hear all the waters of the forest rushing and it filled my years with a tremendous sound.'[81]

Within Devlin's rounding of the two texts, comparisons are made between private and public worlds, between illusion and reality, and between gendered oppositions, which are the source of discrepancies and conflict. Most emphatic is the distinction between patriarchy and its opposition by the lives of women within these texts. The confusion and pain, textually exemplified, are matched by Devlin's artistry, which imposes an order upon disorder, a cohesion upon chaos. Lojek has cited Seamus Heaney's formula, and it is entirely pertinent to Devlin and quoted here in relation to *Ourselves Alone* and *After Easter*: 'The quarrel between free creative imagination and the constraints of religious, political and domestic obligation'[82] becomes, as Lojek states, the quarrel that Devlin resolves textually, and within Greta's psyche. She has managed to escape on the one hand, and to understand the limitations of freedom on the other. It is the integrity of escape and its essential follow-through, the process of assimilation and exorcism, that are central. In form and language, Devlin has demonstrated the religious, political and, indeed, domestic circumstances which have deterred lives from fruition and which, in another sense, relate back to a form of Ulster theatre which she formally repudiates.

In *After Easter* the language and ontology of Rose, in their distinction from the contemporary, recall a more traditional mode of discourse which belongs to the homes, hearths and kitchen sinks of an earlier era in Ulster theatre. In undermining traditional form, and introducing highly contemporary lives, Devlin is highlighting difference. Form and language engage to usurp an earlier naturalistic mode of presentation whose texture could not contain the ideological issues or imaginative extremes that are represented in these texts. Rose represents simplicity and conformity to hegemony, while all else within Devlin's work disputes it. It is a vindication of the death of old terminologies and myths relating to the female. It is an assertion of real women, not altogether perfect, but striving for voice and social acknowledgement.

These texts, *Ourselves Alone* and *After Easter*, present an integrity of imagination and a cultural honesty that prefigure later political developments. Anne Devlin herself has said that, for her, *After Easter* represents a 'female universe in Ireland'.[83]

Conclusion

Some male commentators from the South of Ireland suggest that women playwrights in the North have benefited from a UK axis.[84] In fact, the North's record is indefensible and few signs of nurturing the woman playwright have emerged in the three decades of conflict. It is hardly a cause for pride that from the 1970s to the end of the 1990s only three women have become known or established as Northern Ireland playwrights. Gender considerations pale into insignificance within managements constructed to deliver commercial value and which have shown little evidence of appreciation of the positive power of theatre within society. The political vacuum, which has been created and inhabited almost wholly by men, is matched by a theatre establishment that has been controlled by men. The female voice has been foreign and easily dismissed, whether in theatre or in politics in Northern Ireland.

It is hardly surprising that it is the community theatre movement which fosters women writers who, like those in Charabanc Theatre Company, may achieve and feel confident within collaborative frameworks. This is the fortuitous background of Marie Jones, who perhaps may never have written a word without the initial cooperation and encouragement of mentors and peers alike. The women in community theatre in Northern Ireland do not have to enter competitions or hire agents in order to progress.

Anne Devlin, Marie Jones and Christina Reid share the urban landscape of Belfast. They also share a politic, while representing and interrogating differing political perspectives, whether they be nationalist, republican, unionist or loyalist. Their voices merge in a single statement, which transcends identities based on religion, education or even gender. While all three incorporate gender issues in their work, their ideologies reach beyond those definitions and stretch towards new language, new modes of being and new constructions of society. They are endeavouring to find forms and mechanisms of expression that may contain their visions. They have, at the very least, conveyed the views of women and *their* views of women's lives within Northern Ireland, which is not always an exact equation. Devlin summarises the collective voice the trio presents:

> We are, all of us, disparate communities, at home within it
> when we are ill at ease with everything else. I believe that in
> voicing our differences in our books and plays and poems we
> are already building the peace.[85]

Devlin, Jones and Reid contradict cultural hegemony. While terms such as 'pluralism' and 'inclusivity' dominate current political parlance in Northern

Ireland, their effective reality is remote. Misogynist voices thunder on into the new millennium: Jack's 'Women! Women!... The root of all evil!' (Reid);[86] Malachy's 'I'll leave you alone alright. I'll leave you so you wish you've never been born' (Devlin);[87] and Marty's 'I've been here 25 years, haven't I? The train robbers didn't get that long ... I've never lifted a hand to you yet ...' (Jones).[88] Again, we are reminded of Edgerton's lonely woman who sits silent, 'staring at four walls', while her husband is in the club, 'talking about when he was in Long Kesh'.[89]

While the concept of 'feminisation' must be central to the parlance of 'pluralism' and 'inclusivity' within the context of Northern Ireland, its realisation seems a long way off. In the meantime, we can only work towards an environment in which 'the girls' no longer have to struggle for a part in 'the big picture'.

6 Frank McGuinness
The war in the heads, the war on the streets[1]

I hope that you understand the inclusion of yourself as a male playwright in a book entitled The Girls in the Big Picture. *I suppose I am asking you to vindicate the title in relation to the gendered nature of your work and the need, as I see it, for your inclusion.*

When *The Factory Girls* first opened, I got a card from Mo Toal, the original Ellen, congratulating me as the greatest factory girl of them all. This was a high compliment. I'm proud to say that I play football like a girl but I can drink like a woman, an Irishwoman at that. In the words of Lizzie Burns, when it comes to gender, 'I wish we could all take it aisy.' There is far more fun to be had in muddying rather than separating the issues of male and female, and if sexuality loses its capacity to change and confuse, I've lost interest in it. I feel no need to vindicate my inclusion in *The Girls*, but I think it would be strange if my work were not in it.

Your early life is documented in Margo Harkin's insightful documentary Clearing the Stage *for BBC. There is a gap between childhood and your first play,* The Factory Girls. *Were there other efforts in between? What compelled you to write and what were your early influences?*

Dusty Springfield, Tennessee Williams, Cilla Black, Arthur Miller, Marianne Faithfull, Henrik Ibsen, Simone Signoret, Montgomery Clift, Seamus Heaney, Patsy Cline, Katherine Mansfield, Velvet Underground, Jane Austen, Anton Chekhov, Shakespeare, Joyce, Old English poetry, David Bowie, Flaubert (I've read *Madame Bovary* in French), Eugene O'Neill, Terence Rattigan, Laurel and Hardy, William Carlos Williams, Caravaggio. They all compelled me to write and most of them I discovered as a child/teenager. Television transformed my life. It taught me to read more widely than conventional education ever did. I owe an immense debt to popular music. My first attempts at writing were song lyrics. The fact that I could not read or write music never stopped me.

Your work has often been misinterpreted. There is a strong subtext – in critical theory, we bring our own baggage and respond accordingly. Dido sums it up perfectly at the end of Carthaginians: *'What happened? Everything happened, nothing happened, whatever you want to believe, I suppose.' Some critics, mostly male, miss the point.*

It is frequently the job of critics to miss the point and I am not being facetious here, because at times something very interesting can emerge in predictable dialogue between critic and writer. That is why I have genuine time for the few critics who are not massaging their own ego or displaying their ignorant arrogance when they try to make sense of what they've seen and heard in a play. I think I'm pretty strict with a text before it goes on stage. This means the first few weeks of rehearsal are ruthless in the way I scrutinise every line, every gesture – any director or actor I've succeeded in working with will confirm that. Naturally, I expect eventually an equal ruthlessness on their part with regard to their work and, for actors, that emerges in performance through the run of the play. What I'm really saying is, we are ultimately our own critics, and we have to be if we're to sustain ourselves and survive.

Specifically, the response to the RSC's production of Mary and Lizzie, *one of my favourite plays, was hostile. English critics are well used to anti-colonialist themes from Irish writers. Is it a play beyond its time? Can the critics 'kill' a play?*

Nobody liked the play at the time it was performed. They were wrong. There are things in *Mary and Lizzie* that I admire. That was a hard birth. Still they're with me. Two of my dearest children. No, the critics cannot kill a play. They kill a production.

We've talked about misrepresentation. The corollary may also be true – a sort of academic overkill. The articles and publications are now numerous and well-earned. What is your overview?

I'm an academic myself and proud to come out as such. In answering your question, I think of Miss Prism from *The Importance of Being Earnest*. Her definition of fiction, 'the good ended happily, the bad unhappily', has always been an inspiration. I'm often tempted to go in search of at least a sample chapter of her three-volume novel of more than usually revolting sentimentality. I do not do so and this should be a warning to us all. Had Miss Prism's novel been published, I'm sure numerous articles and publications would have followed. Think what this might have led to. Another three-volume novel or, indeed, a career in politics like Danton.

What about the North, the awful question?

The North is the North is the North. Anyone who tells you they have left it is lying. It is there in everything I write, especially when it does not seem to be there. Theatre is conflict and disguise, war and peace. How could I not write about the war, the peace?

Your adaptations have been spectacularly successful – A Doll's House, Peer Gynt, Uncle Vanya, *to name a few. Why do they attract so little academic attention?*

The plays themselves attract little academic attention. I'm glad of that because I don't want to know what they're about. The theatre is fun, all about playing, and the versions are part of the wonderful craic. Learning is lovely. I learn from the plays I do versions of, and love those authors. For me, that is sufficient. Everything I write I owe to the writers who help me structure, sentence, shape a play.

Introduction

The feminine voice is not the preserve of the female, although separatist feminist movements have long argued that a male cannot produce feminist work. The film critic Annette Kuhn allows the male houseroom when he has wandered in accidentally, unintentionally. In his unconscious travels, it is a feminist reading rather than intentional textual content or meaning that credits male feminism.[2] This position seems as sexist as that which feminism purports to highlight. For other feminist critics, the empirical sex of the author is less important than the sex of the writing produced. Declan Kiberd argues that some modernist masterpieces of Hardy, Lawrence, Joyce and the later Yeats have provided the foundations for feminist criticism and feminine writing. In other words, his claim might be that feminine writing originated in the male-written literature of the early twentieth century and was appropriated by the feminism of the 1970s and 1980s.[3]

Certainly, the belief that men are incapable of intentionally feminine writing would necessitate rejecting much of a key Modernist masterpiece, Joyce's *Ulysses*. Joyce attempted to demonstrate, by means of Molly Bloom's soliloquy, that feminine thought is significantly different from that of the male, and, in his work in general, he adopted a consciously feminine approach. In the character of Leopold Bloom for example, Joyce succeeded in producing a convincing portrait of a new type of man, the feminine man who abhors nationalism, violence and hatred and espouses compassion, generosity and tenderness.

The influence of the Modernist or later Revivalist movement in the South of Ireland eluded the ULT, which created a safe intellectual haven within its citadel. There are no feminine men or feminine work within the annals of the ULT, and there is certainly no evidence of local debate on the possibilities or potential of Modernism as a broad cultural construct. The promotion of sectarianism denied access to any form of enlightenment or Modernism.

Theatre in Northern Ireland had little ideology to fall back on when it was forced to face the realities of a sectarian war in the 1970s and 1980s.

It was in the late 1980s that a new voice emerged in Ulster theatre, challenging extant form and language and a range of hegemonies that had circumscribed creative expression for decades. A male playwright championed the rights and lives of ordinary women and promoted the politics of gender as integral and homogeneous within social constructs. In *The Factory Girls* (1982) there is an outpouring of previously unspoken, half-realised, boiling resentment. Perhaps the women of *The Factory Girls* are the female equivalent of Thompson's shipyard men in *Over the Bridge*. They also precede their cross-border Belfast counterparts of Charabanc's *Lay Up Your Ends* (1983).

The belief in the redemptive power of the feminine lies at the heart of the work of Frank McGuinness, who places himself directly in the tradition of Joyce's Bloom when he says, 'It would only be through a recognition and reappropriation of the feminine principle that revolution in both society and literature could take place.'[4] It is exactly this 'recognition and reappropriation' that is given dramatic form in the plays of McGuinness, particularly in the plays of female absence – *Observe the Sons of Ulster Marching Towards the Somme* (1986) and *Someone Who'll Watch Over Me* (1992) – but also in plays such as *Carthaginians* (1988) and *Mary and Lizzie* (1989), which introduce the possibility of dialogue between masculine and feminine.

McGuinness sees himself, and may be perceived, as both a Northern and an Irish playwright, and his background, born in Buncrana, County Donegal, with Derry as his natural hinterland, makes border crossings a fact of his early life and, in his work, a metaphor for political, social and gender transitions. His subject matter and locations alone identify him with both territories, North and South, which are more intellectual and cultural than literal domains. The sense of always belonging to broader communities allows him to combine and transcend particular borders, and those of theatre North and South. His work may be seen as a contemporary version of the very principles which informed the founding objectives of the ULT, based on liberty, equality, fraternity.[5] At the same time, it presents a contrast to Irish dramatic tradition. Beckett's nihilism or Friel's nostalgia for lost traditions is contested by McGuinness's consistent and unfashionable meliorism

– Lizzie Burns in *Mary and Lizzie* actually describes herself as 'Utopian'. So, too, the dystopian tones of northern playwrights such as Graham Reid and Gary Mitchell contrast sharply with McGuinness's predilection for the combination of the poetic and the vernacular, the potential of language matching the human potential he portrays within the texts. He does not slot into either tradition comfortably, but perhaps provides a new focus for both.

Although many of his characters speak in authentic Derry/border demotic, their dislocation from normal social structures and behaviour invokes criticism of these and suggests as-yet unconstructed futures. In these plays there are no conventional family units and no traditional or contemporary hearths. The contemporary Ulster theatre settings of living room, club or pub are absent. Lost social outcasts create new formations outside the security of tradition: actively, like the rebellious women in *Carthaginians*, naïvely, as in *The Factory Girls*, or passively and involuntarily, like the men in the plays of female absence. In a Donegal factory, a Derry graveyard, a cell in the Lebanon or the trenches of the Somme, authoritarian force is challenged by the reality of ordinary people who are no longer able to endure regimes of suffering. McGuinness isolates his characters in locations that are removed from everyday society, in order that they may question and come to terms with social regimes which are mostly unidentifiable but govern their lives. His starting point is always that of a situation beyond individual comprehension or control. Would-be soldiers arrive at a training camp where there are no trainers, professional people find themselves in a Middle East prison cell, and three men and three women camp out in a graveyard. He uses these abnormal situations to push his characters towards recognition, and even re-creation, of their own identities and catharsis through that experience.

McGuinness's first play, *The Factory Girls*,[6] introduces concepts of feminism and attempts to free women whose situation is impossibly locked within a patriarchal framework. The play provides an introduction to techniques by which McGuinness will progress towards an understanding and absorption of a feminine principle.

The Factory Girls: Feminism as Fantasy

In *The Factory Girls* McGuinness focuses on the confrontation of five women with management and union to assert their right to work in an industry that has been threatened by imports from abroad. The play is set in his home town of Buncrana. Its geographical proximity to Northern Ireland is reflected in the similarities of ethos and politics which affect working lives. The post-war categorisation of women as mothers and home-makers and the subsequent downgrading of traditional female work in the linen mills and shirt factories form the sociological background to the play. As Monica McWilliams, in describing a 'male-stream' culture, points out, 'The State's alignment with the Church helped to institutionalise some of the most extreme forms of patriarchy with a development strategy that would attract investment for male employment.'[7] The expediency of female employment during the war years could conveniently become a cultural dysfunction in the following decades, a dysfunction that could challenge the traditional ideology of church and state. While McGuinness's play contests patriarchal models, his characters are bound by conflicting realities, personal and political, rational and intuitive, religious and communal, to create contradictions that become central themes which the play itself cannot disentangle. The play struggles to find a feminist form within which to contain its feminist theme, exactly as Devlin tries to achieve form in which to contain her women's ambitions and, indeed, her goals as playwright in *Ourselves Alone*. By locating and giving dramatic voice to another set of women's lives, McGuinness, like Devlin, presents the bigger picture of patriarchy which the text may not contain.

The women, who have worked in the factory for years, have been issued new targets by management. They are expected to produce more and increase quality at the same time. Ellen, who has worked thirty years in the factory, is ringleader and finds refuge in this role, which helps to dispel the private loss of her three children, who died within the space of one year. She is official spokeswoman and has fought many battles with the Union. Given the new regime, the women workers decide to take action. The takeover of the manager's office is led by Ellen as a tactic to facilitate negotiation and humiliate Rohan, the manager. It is when Ellen naïvely telephones the new priest to ask him to say mass for the women on Sunday that she realises the full political relevance of her actions and resultant ostracisation by church and community. Subsequently, Ellen's motivation is shown as deeply personal and suspect, as the younger Rebecca emerges as the true feminist:

> REBECCA: Is it because we're too scared to stand on our own
> two feet? You want us scared, Ellen. You think and we
> think that if you take away your hand we'll fall on our
> faces. This time you're not on your own. We're in this
> together.[8]

Rebecca interrogates Ellen's hierarchy, as much as Ellen interrogates that of male management. Ellen, however, reasserts her leadership: 'You should know me by now, daughter. I'm a tougher nut to crack than the other boyos.'[9] But perhaps this is dignity in the face of, and in acknowledgement of, defeat of leadership. The women's final victory is in fantasy and the fantasy of freedom. Rosemary, the youngest of the women, has claimed that she'd rather 'have a horse than get married'.

Rebecca and Rosemary together 'neigh' to push back the barrier on the door, and perhaps metaphorical barriers, with 'one almighty heave', signalling new birth but within a literal defeat. They will fight the good fight against the male hegemony of husbands, management, Catholic church and community. As single young women, the future is certainly not theirs, but it is still worth fighting for. If there is no future for the factory itself, or for the tradition of female employment, which the play highlights as truly exploitative, the older women, Ellen and Una, 'will be carried' to their 'grave squealing' for dignity and self-esteem, which have rarely been credited to them.

The device of 'the party' or 'carnival',[10] which is deployed in McGuinness's later plays to effect communal bonding and dramatic comic interlude, here disintegrates into communal drunken bickering. The symbolic psychic journeys, so painfully traversed in later plays, jolt and start towards the finale of *The Factory Girls*. Fintan O'Toole recognises that the play moves into a new mode towards the end, one which 'goes against the naturalistic grain of the rest of the play and is neutered by it'.[11] McGuinness has employed the dominant theatre form of naturalism to contest a dominant ideology that subverts women. It is when the play takes on the further complexity of internal power struggle that naturalism cannot contain it. There are no internalised redemptions or healings and the friction which is discovered outside becomes another kind of friction among the women within the orbit of their own siege.

The background of male collusion and complicity is spelt out textually, the telephone conversations with the priest and Vera's husband contrasting with the female support offered by outside friend Susan, and the underlining of the terminology 'factory girls' by Vera to manager Rohan: 'not factory women, factory girls. Factory girls never grow old and they don't fade away.' Both Rohan and Bonner refer to the women in deprecating terms of animal imagery: 'hyenas, wildcats and lapdogs'. Against this background, woman emerges as subject, to struggle out of silence: first Ellen and then Rebecca, to whom the mantle is passed, as a younger, more radical generation heralds social change.

As the inscription of Olive Schreiner's poem, as epigraph to the text, highlights, love denies freedom but the latter safeguards both:

I saw a woman sleeping. In her sleep she dreamt Life stood before her and held in each hand a gift – in the one Love, in the other Freedom.
And she said to the woman, Choose.
And the woman waited long and she said Freedom
and Life said, Thou hast well chosen. If thou hadst said Love, I would have given thee that thou didst ask for, and I would have gone from thee and returned to thee no more. Now the day will come when I shall return. In that day I shall bear both gifts in one hand.
I heard the woman laugh in her sleep.[12]

Freedom, however, never becomes realised within the text.

McGuinness has, with compassion and empathy, signified the social, political and domestic subjugation of women within one period in history. But as Tracy C. Davis states:

Women's subject matter does not necessarily make a feminist play, and that unless challenges to form AND content converge, conventional dramaturgy can perpetuate and replicate the ideology of domination even when the playwright's personal view ... is one of abhorrence.[13]

This is almost a summation of McGuinness's first stage play, in which freedom only becomes possible within the realms of fantasy and male hegemony is maintained. McGuinness foresees the feminist struggle's emergence from that period. He has yet to find a feminist form within which to contain it.

Workshop Strategies Towards Text

McGuinness's workshop process presents an insight into the dramatic methodology of the texts which have been informed by the process – *Caoin* (1989) and *Carthaginians* (1988). In 1989 McGuinness led a one-day workshop for members of the Ulster Youth Theatre. This formed his introduction to the young cast, who would eventually perform a commissioned short piece as part of a larger project, based around a dramatisation of Seamus Heaney's poem 'Station Island'.[14] The project was entitled *Stations*,[15] and, as well as McGuinness, writers Mark Brennan, Jennifer Johnston, Robin Glendinning, Michael Longley and Damian Gorman were commissioned by the Ulster Youth Theatre to contribute short pieces, to represent a version of the cultural history of Northern Ireland. Each piece would be interjected between sequences of 'Station Island'. In the workshop, characters were formed, directed, interrogated and led by McGuinness. He created a literal and metaphysical space within which individual dramas became collective, replicating the textual form of *Carthaginians*, *Someone Who'll Watch Over Me* and *The Factory Girls*. Participants were lined up for a marathon race which they would never run.

McGuinness made the setting of the marathon a clearing house, which gave dramatic coherence to disparate psychologies. The physical disengagement from the familiar world, in order to manage it, is a constant device that forms the central structure of most of McGuinness's texts. The manager's office under siege in *The Factory Girls*, the locations of home leave in *Observe the Sons of Ulster Marching Towards the Somme*, the Derry graveyard of *Carthaginians* and the hostage cell of *Someone Who'll Watch Over Me* are all manufactured environments for thematic explorations. The removal of the comforting, or, as it may be, uncomfortable, regalia of everyday functioning provides objective space for personal appraisal and readjustment. Like 'Station Island' itself, personal pilgrimage involves reappraisal of self and its relationship to the collective and communal. Unbeknownst to the participants of his workshop, McGuinness was working towards writing about the Remembrance Day bombing.

The outcome was *Caoin*,[16] a song for nine voices. A poetic elegy for the victims of Enniskillen, *Caoin* is a direct descendant of Synge's keen in *Riders to the Sea*.[17] As in Synge's version of a world turned back-to-front by 'the young men ... leaving things behind for them that do be old', McGuinness sees another literal reversal of life into death:

> A woman in her bridal gown
> Laid out in white, it is her funeral.

Caoin poses the central question of *Carthaginians* and *Observe the Sons of Ulster Marching Towards the Somme* – how do we explain and learn to absorb catastrophe, and how can it begin to be written about, in what shape or form?

In the production of *Stations*, *Caoin* was preceded by a choreographed piece, *The Names*, by Jennifer Johnston. The symbolic linking of the Apprentice Boys of Derry and the dead of Bloody Sunday[18] is made through a roll-call of the names of both sets of men, the device given vogue by Brian Friel in *Faith Healer* (1979) and by McGuinness in *Carthaginians*. The final image of *The Names* is one of a series of pietàs, the women mourning their dead, the women left as ultimate victims, like Synge's Maurya, condemned to a living death, instruments for the absorption of tragedy. The act of the keen, as expressed in McGuinness's text, is an expression of collective mourning and perfectly echoes the scene of collective remembrance where the tragedy actually occurred. On stage, one set of people mourn the deaths of those who had, in life, gathered to mourn the deaths of their immediate kin, the men of the Somme. Of course, too, the subtextual references to *Observe the Sons of Ulster* are there for those who know that play. The keen is pagan, neither Catholic nor Protestant, its practice is female, its ritual collective. The art of the keen is formal and technical. These are apt motifs for the essence of the work of Frank McGuinness.

During the summer of 1986, McGuinness, with Joe Dowling, led a week's workshop for young actors and actresses in Derry. McGuinness has said that he went there with the basis of an idea and that the idea became *Carthaginians*.[19] The group outings to the local graveyard, whose tombstone stories were subsequently re-created, provided textual possibilities. Death was a recurring theme, as were the politics of republicanism and the changing political balance of Derry itself. The final speech of that workshop week suggests the death of one regime and its replacement by another, of which women are the generators and custodians, a symbolically post-colonial future which is founded on a feminist principle:

> This is a magical city, a forbidden city, a city that people are
> frightened of. The city is an empire and the empire is Rome. It
> is a city with ruins and the only way you can find out about it is
> from the ruins and its graveyard. The graves are guarded by
> three women and they hold the power of life as well as
> dominion over the dead. People have visions and they come to
> the women to have them explained. The city is Carthage.[20]

The female custodians of classical mythology are reinstated to link death and life, past and present. The allegory of the empire's destruction of Carthage and the events of Bloody Sunday in Derry is clear. Both rise from the ashes. Like *Caoin,* specific tragedy must be absorbed into history in the construction of new ideologies. This is the site and principle of *Carthaginians*.

Carthaginians: An Ulster Feminist Prototype?

McGuinness has described *Carthaginians* as 'a drama of conversation'.[21] The apparently aimless conversations, which pass the time of waiting from Sunday to Monday in the life of the play (Wednesday to Sunday in the revised text),[22] climb over each other in a highly choreographed dance of language and meaning. 'The wit and wisdom of Derry town'[23] echo through the graveyard, where the six characters have sought asylum from their individual inner mayhem and the public mayhem outside the gates. They harbour 'the memory of wounds',[24] which only a miracle can alleviate. The outward drama of waiting for the dead to rise is paralleled by the inward drama of personal resurrections. Jokes, stories and quizzes rattle on in naturalistic theatrical engagement to relieve the central abstraction of intense and relentless grief.

   To analyse the feminine qualities of the text it is essential to outline the development of the play and introduce its seven characters. Three women sit among the standing stones of a graveyard and a carefully constructed pile of contemporary refuse, beer cans, plastic bags and so on. Maela lays clothes for her daughter's grave. Sarah organises dead leaves and Greta tends a dying bird. These gestures, relating to death, the graveyard setting and the music of Henry Purcell's 'When I am Dead and Laid in Earth', reverberate through the opening dialogue, which moves between idiom and the 'in-between speak', the poetic, which flavours the play:

> GRETA: Anyway, this boy won't live much longer. A goner.
>   Poor old bird. God rest you. God rest us all.
> MAELA: You can only say that over the dead.
> GRETA: We're all dying.
> MAELA: Sarah pet, you'll die of sunstroke if you don't take off
>   that big jumper.[25]

The graveyard is transformed into a picnic site when Dido, Queen of Derry, Queen of Carthage, arrives with his battered pram-load of supplies. Dido is gay, has never done a day's work in his life, according to Maela, and for the graveyard refugees he is the practical link with the outside world, placing bets for Greta and supplying her with cigarettes, as well as the food and other essentials for the sojourn. He has been Maela's partner in pub quizzes – 'Oldie and Goldie' is their pub-quiz title. They share a close relationship despite difference of age and background.

Dido's flamboyant homosexuality lights the play up in a blaze of colour, language and repartee. McGuinness makes him not only a functional but a psychological 'outsider'. He is too young to remember Bloody Sunday, so cannot fully share in the inner experiences of the male and female trios in the graveyard. Dido is a pragmatist, making out, or trying to, financially and sexually. He is clever and streetwise, and for an audience provides relief from the crises that are suffered by the other characters. That is not to say he is immune to suffering; he alone has found mechanisms for its management and an independence and control of his own life, an ability that is lost to the others.

The men drift in, moving gauchely among the women, who have staked their sites for the duration of the play. The women reveal their secrets, their private tragedies, which have brought them to the graveyard. Maela's daughter died of cancer on Bloody Sunday; Greta sings of an imaginary lost brother and of becoming male during menstruation, and she wants to find her lost self-identity; Sarah is recovering from drug addiction. The male secrets emerge later in the play, slowly and through violent confrontation. Hark, in prison, did not join the hunger strike; Seth is an informer; and Paul wishes to join the dead of Bloody Sunday. The men hover around the women. There are pairings of intimacy and confrontation, between Hark and Dido, Hark and Seth, Hark and Sarah, Maela and Seth, and Greta and Hark, leading to the communal activity of the play within the play, Dido's (alias Fionnuala McGonigle's) 'The Burning Balaclava', and the recital of Walter de la Mare's 'The Listeners', which preludes the bonding of the group in the litany of the dead of Bloody Sunday. For the finale of collective exorcism, the seven form a symbolic circle, which brings the play itself full circle back to the language of the opening scene: 'To wash the dead. Bury the dead. Raise the dead. Forgive the dead. Forgive yourself.'[26]

The props of Dido's (Fionnuala's) play are laid to rest. The light breaks and the dawn chorus begins. Like the props, the war in the heads and the war on the streets have been laid to rest. Dido's epilogue reproduces the central metaphor of naming. The names of the living streets, the setting for Maela's nightmare journey of catharsis, substitute the names of their dead: 'Carthage has not been destroyed.'[27] And what has happened in between? In Dido's words: 'Everything happened, nothing happened, whatever you want to believe, I suppose.'[28] The six sleep in peace after the Sunday dawn.

Joe Dowling has said that public lives are most vividly drawn through private agonies.[29] In this text, the significance of Bloody Sunday is traced through the agonies of those who have had to endure life in its aftermath. The centrepiece of the litany of the dead, as one critic describes, 'hangs over the play in an ineradicable pall'.[30] And yet another may state that the play 'is impenetrable . . . for a southerner to follow'.[31] The constant interplay of the literal and the imagined, comic wit and poetry, naturalism and imagism, has made critical reception problematic and inconsistent. David Nowlan shares the discomfort of many critics and cannot accept the lack of explicit detail of the earlier plays:

It is informed by half-realised instincts and local knowledge, which makes the drama less immediately accessible, and the findings of the exploration are a great deal more enigmatic.

Talking of the set, the standing stones and Paul's pyramid of refuse, he makes the case for a naturalistic setting: 'We need to feel more at home to get the full thrust of the messages.'[32]

This hankering for the dominant mode of naturalism and linear development is shared by one critic who declares that the play is 'a bit of a tease so far as plot is concerned, a non-starter for realism, some of its characters are barely outlined and its allegory is farfetched'. And yet, he continues: 'It does work in a strange kind of way.'[33] The difficulty here would seem to be a lack of theoretical knowledge with which to approach the play, an unresolved sense that 'something' is happening but within an alien framework. Lack of empathy with the characters is highlighted as the play's central difficulty. Seamus Hosey complains: 'This mediation leaves one strangely unmoved. We know too little of these characters to care deeply for their plight.'[34] Against this is David Grant's praise: 'Every character displays a completeness which engages our absolute attention.'[35] For Hosey the comic element may be 'unerring' but the play is flawed by the 'tragic symbols of suffering humanity awaiting salvation'.[36] And the opposite view is posed by Michael Radcliffe, that 'the play is flawed by its unfocused comic interludes'.[37] But perhaps the craving for traditionalism and the need to categorise neatly are best expressed by John Peter, who places the play in the tradition of Yeats and Synge, or Beckett:

> I am in two minds about *Carthaginians*. I miss the thrust and heat of confrontation which is so essential to theatre; even in *Waiting for Godot*, an allegedly static play, there's a sense of opposing wills and needs which keeps the play in motion. *Carthaginians*, by contrast, functions as an act of revelation.[38]

But for Robin Thurber, the play is :

> Brilliantly effective and affective. McGuinness's theatrical skill as he lures you, will-o'-the-wisp, into his lurid world, where moments of heightened tragic poetry can be juxtaposed with sharp satire, is breathtaking.[39]

I would argue that a feminist reading of the play can settle these disputes. *Carthaginians* is in constant opposition to the dominant, in form and content, creating what Annette Kuhn terms 'disturbances' to the masculinity of Western discourse.[40] If the masculine attributes of a text are defined as those of 'visibility, goal-orientation, linearity and instrumentality of syntax',[41] these would seem to constitute the very essentials critics find lacking in McGuinness's play. So, too, the multiplicity of meaning, the plurality, as opposed to unity, of the open text may be too problematic for male critics. Only Michael Coveney recognises the sexuality of the text, and its consequent political orientation: 'Sarah Pia Anderson's reverbatively eloquent production sustains the McGuinness metaphor of sexual predilection for political orientation.'[42] The play, which left Hosey 'strangely unmoved',[43] is described by Coveney as 'one of hauntingly coherent beauty and of sadness, and of a deep defiant joy'.[44] The key adjectives 'coherent' and 'defiant' themselves defy the appraisal of the other critics, for whom the play seems flawed because of its (for them) unrecognised feminine qualities. By inference, the diversity of reception to the text, the lack of comprehension of a 'feminist text', may have more to do with the limitations of contemporary criticism than with the work criticised.

Perhaps the most serious misinterpretation of the text was by members of Derry City Council, who promoted a cultural festival, IMPACT 1992, and invited the Druid Theatre Company's production of *Carthaginians*, directed by McGuinness himself. On viewing the play during its Galway run, they declared it to be a travesty of Bloody Sunday and called a special council meeting to consider whether or not to cancel the Derry event.[45]

McGuinness leaves reception open-ended, he refuses to lead his audience into linear, singular interpretation. So, too, he has introduced a binary allegorical format, that of Carthage and the Roman Empire, as related by Paul throughout the play as he builds his pyramid, and the Christian motif of death and resurrection, emphasised by the life of the play in its adherence to the Holy Week schedule, and embodied by Dido as the Christ figure, stoned for his play 'The Burning Balaclava', and making his farewell to his friends/disciples at the end. This double allegory releases the audience from specific conclusions and from moral, fixed meanings, but may give rise to aesthetic frustration for those whose orientation is 'masculine', as witnessed by the critical responses.

McGuinness further underlines his opposition to the dominant by introducing the O'Casey parody, 'The Burning Balaclava'. Its adherence to naturalism cannot embrace complexities of difference, so the continual refrain within that text is to kill – people, dogs, whatever. The formal shortcomings, so cleverly presented by the play within the play, serve as commentary on the contrasting form of *Carthaginians* itself. Its cyclical movement, as Tracy C. Davis might say, 'does not reassure and resolve. It provokes and revolves.'[46] But disturbance is not only formal. It reverberates within the sexuality of the characters themselves and the textual significance of their sexual identities.

Hark is, on the surface, the archetypal male, described as the 'rough man',[47] parading his maleness in aggression and violence. He has left his identity in prison, adopting a new persona, which bears his guilt, naming himself 'Hark' as opposed to Joseph Harkin. His homophobia is pronounced. He responds to Dido's intimate advance, a kiss, with aggression and disavowal. Hark's phallocentrism is contested throughout the text, verbally by Maela and Greta and symbolically by Dido in the sausage scene, where he cajoles Hark, 'Pick a sausage, any sausage',[48] and proceeds to mash them into Hark's face. McGuinness forces Hark, as Victoria White recognises,

> towards the feminine in his relationship with Sarah and the
> consummation of that relationship. In line with the gesture
> towards transcendence, Hark does not absolutely refuse to give
> Sarah a child. The baby is and symbolises man's coming into
> understanding with the feminine.[49]

Hark has a long way to go in understanding the feminine and his fear of it is pronounced. Dido, in comparison, thrives in the full awareness of his own sexual identity. If the men are past defining themselves, Dido's homosexuality is the only constant and certainty within the text. And it is after the uneasy scene between Hark and Dido that Dido's confidence in his sexual identity is asserted and thus steers the play. Dido disturbs fixed perceptions of sexuality to make an audience accept him as the Christ figure.

McGuinness's women represent different aspects of the feminine. They reflect three personifications of the maternal instinct, although all are childless. Maela has lost her daughter and Sarah craves a child. Greta mourns the loss of an imaginary brother and has experienced trauma at puberty, when she thought she was becoming male, the imagined brother. She has had a hysterectomy at an early age and feels that she has lost herself and her femininity. Greta's sexual identity is complex. Of the three women, she is the aggressor who stands up to Hark. She is independent and challenges female stereotyping. (She has converted her mother's 'doll's house' into an untidy home for herself.) McGuinness here signifies more than an independent woman who combines male and female.

In the attention he pays to the biological, to the trauma of puberty and to Greta's confused (if it is confused) sexual identity, McGuinness is forcing analogies, not entirely clear but certainly relating to Freudian theories of the Oedipal and, in turn, the complex area of feminist psychoanalysis. This leads to the issue of gender difference and language, as debated by post-Lacanian feminist theory. Juliet Mitchell in 'Psychoanalysis and Feminism' posits that Freudian theory is not a recommendation for a patriarchal society, but an analysis of it.[50] In turn, the French feminist movement believed that psychoanalysis could provide an emancipatory theory of the personal and a path to the exploration of the unconscious, both of vital importance to the analysis of the oppression of women in patriarchal society.

Lacan's 'mirror image' theory develops Freud's analysis of the Oedipus complex. The child's sight of its image in the mirror is the point of rupture or separation from what Lacan describes as the Imaginary, the pre-Oedipal state (Freud) in which the child believes itself to be part of the mother and perceives no separation between itself and the world. The 'lack' or loss of the mother and the desire for this former existence is repressed to open up the unconscious. The acceptance of this 'lack' coincides with the first acquisition of language and entry to the Symbolic Order, where the phallus substitutes the lack of the mother.[51] In both Luce Irigaray's and Julia Kristeva's analyses, the woman who refuses entry to the Symbolic Order is hysteric (Irigaray) or psychotic (Kristeva).[52] As Toril Moi says of Irigaray:

> The hysteric mimes her own sexuality in a masculine mode,
> since this is the only way in which she can rescue something of
> her own desire. The hysteric's dramatisation of herself is thus a
> result of her exclusion from patriarchal discourse.[53]

Greta relates to the father figure, approaching him for explanation of menstruation. He upholds a male prerogative by sending her to her mother, who spins yarns about fairies. Greta's mother would seem to be 'hysteric' or 'psychotic'; she hides under the table with her 'secrets'. Greta's non-alignment with the mother separates her from a female position of subjugation. The ideological separation from the mother is definite and cultural. It is the psychic separation from imagination that is problematic. Greta's menstrual trauma is an analogy of rupture and of the Lacanian primary repression which separates 'the other' from the genderless state of imagination. Greta 'imagines' she had a brother, who, she says, is 'herself'. So, too, she 'imagines' herself, through her own blood, becoming male:

> I thought I was turning into a man. My bleeding was a sure
> sign. I was certain the next thing after the breasts and the blood
> would be I'd grow a beard. Months afterwards, whenever I was
> lonely, I'd touch my breasts, and say, at least I'll soon have a
> brother and he'll be myself.[54]

In her use of language, Greta represents oppositional discourses. She can mimic or mime, in Irigaray's terminology, the male mode and she is the only one who can match Hark's male idiom. He refers to her as 'a walking monument to the wit and wisdom of Derry town'. She is also expert at the 'in-between speak' referred to earlier: her refrain is an example: 'I have only one brother, may God rest his soul. He was drowned in the river . . . '[55]

Greta is not 'mad', but it is insinuated that Paul probably is. His language and syntax are disrupted, a clear expression of his pain, the parading of which Greta despises. She enlists her masculinity in refusing to display the emotional. Greta's psychic journey is akin to Maela's literal journey through the streets. Maela, however, comes to terms with the reality of her loss. Greta cannot, because hers is the central dilemma of feminist debate: to define is to essentialise, is to become trapped by male logic. In the graveyard she can only meet a vision of herself. She has to learn to embrace the masculine and the feminine more easily within that self.

This androgynous symbiosis is embodied clearly by Dido's homo-sexuality. He is biologically male but embraces the feminine within it and thus, in Lacanian or Kristevian terminology, finds a comfortable place in the

Symbolic Order; one of his many responses highlights his security of gender against the uncertainties of the others:

> I know my kind, Hark. Do you want me to name them? Well,
> there's me. That's all. That's enough. I know how to use what's
> between my legs because it's mine. Can you say the same?
> Some people here fuck with a bullet and the rest fuck with a
> Bible, but I belong to neither, so I'm off to where I belong. My
> bed. On my own. My sweet own.[56]

Here McGuinness is thwarting the patriarchy by which Kristeva would see not only the female but the feminine male marginalised. He has placed Greta firmly on the periphery, between the Imaginary, the Symbiotic and the Symbolic, a genderless state that is neither male nor female. Within this patriarchal scheme, woman may inhabit either boundary of the frontier, the edge closest to the void, Freud's 'dark continent', or that which turns inwards towards the Symbolic to protect it from the void and represent the other unknown, that which is elevated – as Moi puts it: 'The representatives of a higher and purer nature.'[57] McGuinness floats Greta, like an atom in space, around her position of marginality. To return to the earlier analogy, she is exiled in the graveyard in an attempt to enter the Symbolic Order in which Dido has found security of identity. She could well end up as the baglady of the earlier play, whose irreconcilable conflict between love and hate of the father has thrown her back as 'hysteric' into the Imaginary.

As Coveney's summary of McGuinness's 'sexual predilection for political orientation' suggests, *Carthaginians* may be seen as an image of 'forming a new nation',[58] the playwright's own description of the contemporary process of Ireland, North and South. The graveyard itself is a metaphysical landscape, in which the marginalised, male and female, seek psychic and sexual identities in order to understand, come to terms with and manage their lives. In so doing, they form a temporary alternative social order. Masculine privileging of reason, order, unity and lucidity is upset in and by *Carthaginians*. Its complex layers explode male binary systems through form, language and the representations within the text. In turn, critics have been mostly unable to accept the challenges of the text, a situation which McGuinness has tried to rectify in revision and in his own direction of the play for Druid Theatre. These textual revisions are 'small but significant'.[59] Formally, the most radical change is in the reversal of the recital of 'The Listeners' and the litany of the names, which in the rewrite is the finale of the play before Dido's epilogue. This crescendo towards the naming of the dead displaces the characters themselves and their private tragedies to accentuate the momentous public tragedy of Bloody Sunday. In addition, Hark's blessing, in the revised text – 'May perpetual light shine upon you'[60] – not only heightens the liturgical element of the ritual but suggests a new Hark.

Greta's sexuality as portrayed by the first text is, in the second, reduced in complexity, and the feminist allusions are also diminished. In all, the revised text is less universal, more localised in language and representation. This revision is understandable, given the controversy that surrounded the play before its performance in Derry. McGuinness's special, if sentimental, gesture to that particular situation lies in a new final line, solely for Derry audiences:

> DIDO: I love youse all. I love you, Derry.

There are reverberations here of the ULT's predicament, where the original ideology had to capitulate to popular demand. Greta's straightforward presentation of her identity in the revised text underplays, indeed negates, the feminist complexity of her original portrayal, and dilutes the signifiers of feminist content and form.

The play in revision is still a feminist text, however, and still cannot please all the critics. Gerry Colgan adamantly states that his reaction to the first production 'has not been changed by a new production':

> The play's ending does not seek to tie up its numerous loose
> ends. It is, by and large, a work in which the plums are of more
> consequence than the pudding.[61]

But Eamonn Jordan notes in his conclusion to an analysis of *Carthaginians*, 'Meaning is held off and references are not tied up. The spectator should not see this as a failure as the very looseness is central to McGuinness's purpose.'[62] The text is open and McGuinness states this categorically in Dido's 'What happened? . . .'[63]

Both *Carthaginians* and *Observe the Sons of Ulster Marching Towards the Somme* passed the test of controversy, which was instigated in both cases by a localised sense of ownership of history and of particular tragedies within it. The two plays compassionately deal with the specific tragedies (Bloody Sunday and the Somme) to bestow upon them respect and meaning within their temporalities and beyond. It would seem that McGuinness's plays are in a state of constant struggle with not so much public perception as preconceptions of them, and that the controversy is eventually humiliated and annihilated by reception of the text in question. The episode of the tour to Derry by Druid Theatre mirrors that of the Abbey Theatre's production of *Observe the Sons of Ulster Marching Towards the Somme* before it came to the Grand Opera House in Belfast.[64] In both cases, reception vindicated the integrity of the texts and embarrassed those who had so badly misinterpreted them. The problem of preconception becomes a problem of reception in the later play, *Mary and Lizzie*. Its inherent anti-colonial feminism creates good reason for some to dismiss the play without proper justification.

Another Feminist Paradigm

For the first production of *Mary and Lizzie*,[65] the Royal Shakespeare Company chose the aesthetic security of their experimental venue, The Pit, at the Barbican in London. Critical response to the play was at best confused and it seems to have been understood only by a single critic, Richard Allen Cave, who remarked that the play 'caught most British reviewers off-guard. Confused by the challenge of the new that unsettled their expectations, they responded with coldly patronising aloofness to McGuinness's subtly brilliant account of Irish history.'[66]

The thrust of the text is in the interplay of its historical narrative, the journey of the sisters Mary and Lizzie through it, and the power of the feminine psyche, which disrupts and explodes every ideological icon in its path. Hegemonies of empire, religion (Catholic and Protestant), capitalism and Marxism are linked together and crowned by the primal hegemony of patriarchy. While woman is represented as victim, the sisters' confidence in their own sexuality is the revolutionary force which ploughs its way through the carnage of various historic betrayals.

In proceeding from confrontation to confrontation, the play is picaresque. Each of its episodes has a temporal location which is transcended through a dream-like subliminality that universalises specific history and transforms the sisters' ordinary gestures into poetic discourse. Mary and Lizzie dance through this half-real, half-nightmare world of historical cause and effect, refusing to be harnessed by cultural stereotypes of womanhood, rejoicing in their individuality, their sisterhood, their love and freedom. McGuinness creates, through them, a feminist polemic whose revolutionary potential is unlimited in itself, but totally limited by the context in which they operate. They find temporary fulfilment in residence with Engels in Manchester. They delight in outraging Marx, who is represented as eccentric, selfish and neither likeable nor worldly-wise. In McGuinness's text, Marx espouses female emancipation while subjugating his wife. He honours the working class and explicitly hates the poor. It is Marx who is the patriarchal husband running a patriarchal marriage. Finally, a dramatic rupture with Engels espouses radical feminism and separatism as the only course of action for Mary and Lizzie. They reject the male order of rationality and attempts to control identity. They claim the right to *jouissance*, to reason, to desire and to love.

The combination of nature and reason is echoed, too, in the language and formal exegesis of the text. Cave refers to the logic of the action as 'the logic of dream'. Without literally espousing feminist criticism, he almost defines the feminist text: 'Like nightmare,' he says, 'the play has a fierce clarity that disturbs precisely because it is so immediate.' 'It appeals,' he continues, 'to subliminal reaches of awareness in an audience.'[67] So, too, the formal resonances within this text and *Carthaginians* translate Cave's immediacy of nightmare into another context, that defined by Kristeva as Women's Time. Commenting on this Kristevian concept, Alice Jardine states that 'female subjectivity would seem to be linked to cyclical time (repetition) and to monumental time (eternity)'.[68] The formal cycle of *Carthaginians*, from initial to final vision within the graveyard, the repetitions of Greta's refrains and the literal obsessions with reproduction and motherhood place that text within the concept of cyclical time. Kristeva sees linear time as the time of history, or political time, masculine in essence and, in Jardine's words, related to project, teleology, departure, progression and arrival, the beginning and ending, the tying up of loose ends so craved by the critics of McGuinness.

Kristeva outlines another element of time within feminist chronology. She outlines three periods and ideologies, the first demanding equal rights with men – as Jardine puts it, the 'right to a place in linear time'.[69] The second phase, underlining gender difference, demands the right to remain outside linear time, the right to reclaim cyclical and monumental time. Contemporary feminism, Kristeva argues, demands the reconciliation of both times, the linear historical and the monumental, the identity of sexual difference within the given political and historical framework in which it exists. The analogy with *Carthaginians* is clear. The play is set in 1985 and deals with a particular political period, as well as a fixed tragedy within a universal period. In *Mary and Lizzie*, McGuinness juxtaposes linear historic time with cyclical time, embodied by the psyches of the two sisters. The given historical period underlines the universal symbolic time of the eternal subjugation of women, with Mary and Lizzie as symbols of attempts towards emancipation from it, the right to remain outside linear time.

Within the linear temporality of the graveyard in the 1980s, McGuinness subsumes historical time into the cyclical or monumental time of the myth of resurrection, in Kristeva's words creating an 'all-encompassing and infinite like imaginary space'[70] around characters whose existence is at once literal and symbolic, and whose orbit is temporal and monumental. This is the principle that particularly governs the text of *Mary and Lizzie*. While the sisters traverse linear time, they communicate with 'a city of women'[71] who live in the trees. These are the dispossessed, those jilted by centuries of colonialism, abused by British soldiers. The linear blends again with the monumental when Mary and Lizzie meet the women from the Russian camps at the end of the play. Their history blends with the history of their Irish peers and the journey of Mary and Lizzie enters the true frame of the 'monumental'. Particular history is absorbed in both *Mary and Lizzie* and *Carthaginians* into a universal or 'monumental' time frame, within which specific locations of linear time both achieve and shed their importance. The texts become instances of formally dramatised feminist ideology.

Female Absence and Male Bonding

Where the women of the trees and camps in *Mary and Lizzie* represent the historic victims of colonialism as feminine, female absence in *Observe the Sons of Ulster Marching Towards the Somme* and *Someone Who'll Watch Over Me* presents a more complex challenge in terms of gender and feminist exposition. In *Observe the Sons of Ulster*, woman is the object of male contempt and in *Someone Who'll Watch Over Me* women are background figures in the form of Edward and Michael's wives. In *Someone Who'll Watch over Me*, Edward's inherent (and educated) nationalism is as closed as the loyalism of his counterparts in *Observe the Sons of Ulster*. In the first play, Edward is a journalist from Northern Ireland, taken hostage in the Lebanon. He is forced to accept difference when he is joined by another hostage, Michael, who is English, a university lecturer and a widower. In the second, the Ulster soldiers have to accept Pyper, who is upper class, an artist, and shares neither accent nor political orientation with the other men. In both texts McGuinness incorporates changing attitudes towards the feminine as analogous to the private transformations that occur within these male psyches. The extreme masculine/loyalist culture of the sons of Ulster not only excludes woman but associates her with 'Papishness', and 'Papishness' with femininity, sectarianism inextricably bound with sexism. Pyper's story of the 'Papish whore'[72] who had three legs is believed by Moore, who says that he has only heard it before in relation to nuns. Anderson, one of the two Belfast representatives of the eight volunteers, addresses the gathering as 'ladies' as he 'spies a Taig',[73] and McIlwaine's outlandish impression of Patrick Pearse is as an effeminate man: 'He was a Fenian. No soldier. Fenians can't fight. Not unless they're in a post office or a bakery or a woman's clothes shop. Disgrace to their sex!'[74] And so, Fenians are weak and feminine, loyalists strong and masculine. McGuinness equates masculinity with naïveté, cliché, reductionism and the ready-made certainties of a Protestant ethos.

David Nowlan sees *Observe the Sons of Ulster* as 'one of the most comprehensive attacks ever made in the theatre on Ulster Protestantism'.[75] Joseph O'Connor contests this view, saying, 'It is not an attack on Ulster Protestantism. It is an urgent communication of insight into the nature of political ideologies and allegiances.'[76] Cavan Hoey sees the alleged 'attack on Ulster Protestantism' as 'reductive and distorting'.[77] In a sense there is truth in both viewpoints, but the text goes further than either acknowledges, in that it works to outline a social and spiritual tyranny that eventually the soldiers, in their moments of self-realisation, must understand and react against. At the training camp and the Somme, leadership is as faceless as the faceless and exploitative ethos that has brought them there to be slaughtered, not to die for Ulster but to be the ultimate 'sacrifice'.[78] They move from fixed ideologies towards a state of anxiety and, ultimately, towards realisation of a huge cultural betrayal. Even the known certainties of geographical rootedness, identity, are questionable as the men are isolated from their local identities at the sites of home leave, the rope bridge, the Tyrone church, the field at Edenderry (Belfast site of the Twelfth celebrations). They have become the dispossessed with only each other to fall back on.

McGuinness exploits the Protestant obsession with place, which, as Declan Kiberd comments within another context, is an 'attempt by those estranged from Catholic spirituality and nationalist history to find in geography a home for their insecure sense of Irishness'.[79] Away from Ulster, the men keep a tenacious grip on it. Back home, in Part 3, this identification with place has been undermined and the men are left with only symbols and emblems of place. Their world, as manifested by rootedness in place, has dissolved, as McIlwaine expresses it at the Twelfth field:

> McILWAINE: It's no good here on our own. No good without
> the bands, no good without the banners. Without the chaps.
> No good on our own. Why did we come here to be jeered
> at? Why did we come here, Anderson?
> ANDERSON: To beat a drum.[80]

On home soil, alone with their emblems, the men confront their common crises. Fear of the inevitable turns the war in their heads and the war in the trenches into a nightmare vision of desolation, betrayal and disassociation. The volunteers become a microcosm of a Protestant dispossessed, as lost and helpless at home as in the no-man's-land of the Somme and as their Catholic counterparts of the Derry graveyard in *Carthaginians*. As the men move towards a useless catharsis, McGuinness echoes other commentators on the Protestant ethos.

Historian Marianne Elliott and United Kingdom Unionist Party leader Robert McCartney both elaborate on the exploitation of an ethic whose political and cultural adherences are betrayed by the very forces to which they adhere, loyalty to the Crown, to Britain. Elliott sees that 'one part of the nation seems content to remain in a sort of willing servitude, merely to lord it over another part' (Elliott is referring to loyalists 'lording it' over nationalists).[81] McCartney's summary serves McGuinness's text well: 'To make the will of authority the will of the people is to establish the triumph of despotism by forcing the slaves to declare themselves free.'[82] This sense of betrayal, of enslavement, is voiced by Pyper and dealt with dramatically throughout the text. The elder Pyper's prologue embodies the central contradiction within the Protestant ethos ('the triumph of despotism'):

> Answer me why we did it, why we let ourselves be led to extermination? . . . That is not loyalty. That is not love. That is hate. Deepest hate. Hate for oneself.[83]

So, too, the volunteers move towards an increasingly intuitive notion of their own exploitation and, in so doing, must question their hereditary beliefs.

Helen Lojek describes Pyper as an 'outsider',[84] not only by virtue of his sexual orientation and class difference but by his own rationalisation and willed exemption from a society he has viewed as closed. Textually, his homosexuality provides a privileged instrument for analysis and, as Lojek states, 'provides a perspective not a theme'.[85] But it is a central perspective, because the volunteers, immediately recognising and repudiating Pyper's homosexuality, silently endorse difference by electing him leader and mentor. In so doing, they have moved towards identification without the ability to rationalise the shift in perspective. These men have found some kind of psychic status even if they cannot fully understand it or equate with it, a status that has allowed them the emotional will to discover Pyper's truth, which they recognise as more legitimate than their own. They are too entrenched in values which have enslaved them and their people for centuries to move towards any real enlightenment or new ideology. But they do perceive that their certainties have been diminished. In turn, too, Pyper descends from his outsider status to identify with them. They all shift towards a new order, in which their differences have been diluted and are certainly less important than at the beginning of the play. Even Roulston, who makes himself an outsider by his fundamentalist literalism and constant reference to the Bible, may capitulate to the radical Pyper to ask him to preach and say the final prayer.

As in *Carthaginians*, a meta-community has found its own brand of truth and in that discovery has had to shift positions, positions which have been historically and ideologically fixed by external forces. The essential difference between these journeys of enlightenment is that for one (*Carthaginians*), new life dawns, for the other (*Observe the Sons of Ulster*), life becomes an impossibility. Eventually, Pyper the outsider becomes the insider. As sole survivor, his life becomes a living death and one dedicated to the memory of his comrades and to the ethos of 'no surrender'. Echoing his parodies of the early acquaintance with these comrades, he joins, in his own terms, 'God's chosen'.[86]

Identity has been challenged and confronted and, in the words of Philip Orr, there has been 'a breaking of the silence'. His documentary *The Road to the Somme* analyses the silence which was the Ulster response to exploitation and Ulster's own self-censorship of the events and their aftermath. Almost in the language of McGuinness, Orr states:

> A strident espousal of glory, traditions, sacrifices and absolutes is entirely different in tone from the mundane but authentic voice of the ordinary human being whom circumstances threw into the crucible of violence. Ulster Protestants must make a careful choice about which voice they prefer to listen to, and which kind of history to challenge.[87]

McGuinness's 'kind of history' challenges traditional absolutes and thereby breaks the silence.[88] The men must accept that they have been led, untrained and unprepared, to a slaughter. In turn, reception must admit and recognise not only the waste and human carnage of war but the particular and perhaps unnecessary loss of life, a sorer reality than that of the glory of sacrifice, a soothing myth that makes the awful reality more endurable.

McGuinness's text becomes a kaleidoscope of scenarios challenging ideology, the fears, disenchantments represented by the scenes of home leave and compared starkly to the relative peace shared by Craig, the recruit from Fermanagh, and Pyper, and symbolised by the two-faced standing stones of Boa Island. (As the men return home for leave, Craig has invited Pyper to spend the time with him in Fermanagh and they visit Boa Island to look at the standing stones and to share the isolated beauty of the place. They share emotional closeness, which may be sexual. The standing stones have two faces, back and front, and represent sexual duality.)

The reversal of myth in the enactment of the Battle of Scarva[89] and the reversal of history by an act of horseplay within it are beyond the comprehension of the men. That William falls from his horse can barely be contemplated by them. They rush towards avoidance, towards the smell of the Somme and the ultimate enactment of myth, the belief that they are on home ground, fighting for their own territory. McGuinness underlines the masculine interpretation of myth and subverts it by allowing his protagonists the escape of fantasy within it. Their original 'blood lust' has become a death wish. Like their female counterparts in *The Factory Girls* and *Carthaginians*, reality is too difficult to bear and radical change is far beyond the limited power of their individual human resources.

McGuinness's challenge to given perceptions of Ulster and of its Protestantism operates within a framework that allows individual and collective triumph alongside deeply felt tradition. That tradition is masculine in essence and, to legitimise itself, must open to the feminine qualities this text endorses. It begins and ends in ideology and personal lives, which are uncertain and must be questioned. But the real questioning remains subtextual and the characters themselves, as indeed Orr has confirmed, are unable to face the truth that history too has also been unable to accept another version of heroism. The ambiguity of the final affirmation of dispossession, 'the temple of the Lord is ransacked ... Ulster', suggests that there is recognition and, at the same time, denial, a falling back on well-worn ideology. The text therefore questions and also allows the honour of commemoration. Perhaps McGuinness has offered the rationale for that 'ransacking' and, within this text, given credence to both the preservation of the values of inherited Protestantism and its contemporary interpretations. To break through the surface of iconography, these men have broken down barriers between themselves, and between their regional and their cultural and political identities. We find them, at the end, *almost* ready for a new beginning.

Eventually, real and metaphysical barriers blur, so that when McGuinness sends the men 'over the top', it is an image so powerful in its connotations and so poignantly literal in its realism that its reception may be as diverse as the varieties of disillusionment suffered by the men. McGuinness formalises and gives space to the ritual, which can be mythologised. He gives greater space to the reality of deaths, which are unwarranted. Both operate in tandem and offer diverse receptions. The elegy for the sons of Ulster or the interrogation of the autocracy, which has informed their meagre lives and sent them to early deaths, offer dual responses and readings. The dignity of myth is preserved and the challenge to colonialism is proffered. The march towards the Somme may be seen as the march towards wilful self-destruction and the inability to chose life.

Jordan states that McGuinness needed to end the play chanting the name of the province 'Ulster'. McGuinness has said that he did not want to let the men die.[90] But eventually he is driven towards capitulation, towards an apparent gesture of acceptance of mythologies which have been interrogated throughout the play. The men and audience alike have been forced to inter-rogate the masculinity of fixed identities, which are grounded in a mixture of myth and prejudice. McGuinness's reinstatement of heroic death for Ulster provides contradictions and readings that are ambivalent and feminist in essence. In reception the choice of meaning and its reverberation is open-ended. He does not upset an audience whose allegiances have been to the men of Ulster, although he disturbs fixed perceptions, and he does not guar-antee solace to anyone. Similarly, he does not totally undermine an ethos that has underpinned cultural values. He leaves it with respectful questioning and with a deep understanding of its significance.

McGuinness's text pushes private relationships and their revelations into a highly public sphere. Seemingly small and personal disillusionments build to threaten the public image of death for a cause, of lives exchanged for a better future. Finally, the audience, like the men, have choices, to accept the 'dark-ness' within the text, the portrayal of the 'despotism' at the heart of loyalism. Or the text may be read as a poignant and fitting memorial to the bravery of the men of the 36th Ulster Division.

The dramatically manufactured and historically correct location of the Somme gives way to that of the Beirut hostage cell in *Someone Who'll Watch Over Me*.[91] If masculinity has been a theme of *Observe the Sons of Ulster*, it is the interrogation of masculinity that is the theme of *Someone Who'll Watch Over Me*. The play debates and defines masculinity within a literal framework of imprisonment, within the characteristic setting of

McGuinness's work – environments that are removed from reality in order to question and understand it.

The American, Adam, and Irishman, Edward, are joined in captivity by Englishman, Michael. In *Observe the Sons of Ulster*, where McGuinness creates a representational map of Northern Ireland by placing the regional duos in a geographical crescent around the stage, with a matter of a few actual miles creating distances of difference and of identity, so, too, this crescent shape is drawn by Adam (stage right), Edward (centre stage) and Michael (stage left). Chained to their positions, these are fixed throughout the play. The cultural representations are obvious, and as the relationships between the men develop, cultural difference is pronounced and challenged. Adam is the least substantially characterised, more a symbol highlighting the symbolic significance of his captivity and the dehumanisation that marks the practice and ideology of the unseen captors. Textually, his presence allows McGuinness to draw the key features of Edward, the 'big boy', the national-ist, whose misogyny is culturally deeply rooted. Edward admits that he does not know his wife or children, that, in Adam's words, he would have married the racing horse Dawn Run 'except she was a Protestant',[92] and he blithely recalls 'screwing' a woman in Omagh one night, only to wake up in the sober light to see that 'she looked like a man'.[93] Edward has as little knowledge of the feminine as his Protestant equivalents, and his propensity for denying female gender is continually underlined. Binary opposition is broken. Educated Catholics are also capable of sexism and sectarianism, even if their expression of it is less obtuse and obvious.

As with *Carthaginians*, stories, jokes and fantasies pass the time of waiting and while the imminence of death is always present and becomes a reality for Adam, it is the psychic journeys and their symbolic reverberations that map themes and subtext. Michael's arrival is dramatically presented by McGuinness in a change of key, reminiscent of Dido's entrance in *Carthaginians* and that of McIlwaine and Anderson in *Observe the Sons of Ulster*. Michael's stereotypical Englishness, his Eton accent and his obsession with his outing to the market 'for pears' to make 'a pear flan' (he had invited some colleagues from the university to dinner so that he might 'learn the ropes') become comic within the closed environment of the hostage cell.[94] He immediately relates all there may be to know about himself, that he has been made redundant as a lecturer in Old and Middle English and has come to teach at the university in Beirut. The inherent irony of the need for such scholarship within a war-torn extremist Muslim–Christian conflict adds to the absurdity, and when his apparent femininity is questioned by Edward, he says that he is widowed but that his mother is still alive.

Jordan's reading of the three characters is exaggerated. He states that they have 'no vocation' and are in Beirut 'for the money'. Certainly, Michael's motives are based on self-interest, but they are not mercenary or exploitative. He 'absolutely needs to work' and that need has been denied him within the restructuring of his English university. Jordan accuses all three of being stubborn, irresponsible and arrogant. Michael's behaviour and actions would seem to be more driven by innocence, which is highlighted by his attempts to transfer the niceties of academe to such a crucible of violence and unrest. Yet he is the epitome of the English gentleman and has tried as best he knows how to integrate and learn about the conflict, a process he exactly repeats within the new situation of the hostage cell. Firmly standing his ground, Michael deflects and demolishes Edward's racist attacks through superior knowledge and education and with a finely tuned rationality which has absorbed some of Edward's colloquialisms and propensity for banter. He is becoming stronger by the minute, while Adam has given up and Edward's bravura is waning. Edward's confusion is at its height when he confidently states: 'They [the captors] do as they're ordered. I do as I choose.'[95] This, in the circumstances, is either a hugely metaphysical statement or the opinion of someone close to the edge of sanity. Adam is as much a political pawn within the textual schema as he is hostage, highlighting the irrationality of the condition of all the hostages. While McGuinness here is developing the relationship of English and Irish, the dissonance of coloniser and colonised, Adam's presence introduces difference and cultural identity as a theme.

The aftermath of Adam's departure, when we assume that he has been shot, and Edward's resulting hunger strike is a signal of cathartic change within the movement of the text and for the characters themselves. Maela's nightmare voyage through the streets of Derry in *Carthaginians*, the discomfort and disassociation of home leave for the men of *Observe the Sons of Ulster* and the collapse of faith for the country-and-western singer of the Marathons workshop are similar preludes to catharsis.[96] These experiences lead to re-newal, or at least its possibility. Edward disintegrates, mentally, spiritually and physically (in his refusal to eat). It is Michael who nurses him towards recovery and new life, which is based on recognition of the fact of Adam's death, but more so on his recognition of life and the necessity of the inclusion of a feminine consciousness within the male psyche.

Michael adopts Edward's role as the instigator of high jinks and fantastic performances. He re-enacts the 1977 Wimbledon Ladies' Tennis Final between Virginia Wade and Betty Stove, contesting every protest from Edward with a speed and wit surpassing Edward's own high-quality repartee. This continues at a breathless pace until Edward has readjusted and entered their world again. He speaks of his wife for the first time and Michael asks whether or not he had slept with Adam or had wanted to. It is a moment of quiet intimacy and of truth and signifies the change in Edward, who has been beaten down, reduced and unable to function as his previous self. Michael has already dealt with trauma, with his wife's death. Edward is an outsider to pain and loss and has little resilience to it.

It is within this context that situations from the other texts combine into collective meaning. Trauma, and the pain of it, lead to enlightenment and a new way of coping with life and living it. This has occurred within the life of all the texts. The grief and private/public suffering within *Carthaginians*, the loss suffered by Ellen in *The Factory Girls* and the terrible loss of the foundations of identity in *Observe the Sons of Ulster* are dramatic experiences which are destined to change and renew lives. Edward, on the other hand, has spent his life painstakingly avoiding any confrontation that might impair his superficial and pleasurable existence. He is also an outsider to any comprehension of the complex sexuality of the world around him. McGuinness introduces Edward to a totally new life in his leave-taking of Michael. This is double-edged, an entry to a living death without Michael, the ambiguous world of the older Pyper in *Observe the Sons of Ulster*, and Edward has learnt enough, we must assume, to sustain himself. He has witnessed the strength and obduracy which Michael, the 'effeminate' Englishman, has displayed, and he has been nurtured by him and by his values.

The farewell gesture when Edward combs Michael's hair is a silent communication of emotion. It signifies the shift in lives that has occurred through the journey of the play. Such a gesture by Edward at the beginning of the play would have been unimaginable. At its finale, he is able to admit to Michael: 'You're the strongest man I know.'[97] The final words of the play are:

> EDWARD: Right, right.
> MICHAEL: Right.
> EDWARD: Good luck.
> MICHAEL: Good luck.

As Michael is left alone, he translates an Old English poem.

> MICHAEL: Whither thou goest, I will go with thee, and whither
>   I go, thou shalt go with me.
> (*Silence*)
>   Right. Right. Good luck.
> (*He rattles the chains that bind him.*)
>   Good luck.[98]

Monosyllabics underscore the length and the depth of the emotional journey travelled by both men and led by Michael. Edward has moved towards some kind of transcendence in his breakdown and has become victim of his own dictum: 'Save us from all those who believe they're right.'[99] He has had to challenge his own beliefs and racial prejudices in accepting an Englishman's sense of values. The personal has been politicised.

The critical response to *Someone Who'll Watch Over Me* was a predictable mixture of praise and reservation, with one critic referring to the play as 'infinitely thinner than *Observe the Sons*'[100] and another describing it as the finest play since *Observe the Sons*.[101] Of all that has been written on *Someone Who'll Watch Over Me*, ironically only ex-hostage Brian Keenan refers to the feminine within the text. He states that McGuinness 'hints at the female echoing in us all',[102] and he summarises the theme of the play: 'that brave men are only so when they recognise the female in themselves'. Employing imagery whose relevance might be totally unconscious, Keenan brings us back in a literal sense to *The Factory Girls* when he describes 'the unseen seam of the feminine sewing the parts together'. This same seamlessness joins all of McGuinness's work within a uniform dramatic strategy.

Conclusion

McGuinness has stated the importance of feminism as an ideology, within the texts and in media interviews. 'All my plays are studies of sexual politics in a way. When I came to be an adult, feminism was a very exciting, very innovative way of perceiving things and that certainly shaped me.'[103] His academic awareness of feminist criticism is borne out by the texts and his own acknowledgement of influences.[104] While Brian Keenan and Victoria White have recognised the feminine impulse within the plays, these influences and their exposition generally lack recognition.

McGuinness has contended that lack of understanding of the feminine is the central weakness of contemporary art, and he has subtly enriched his own art with feminist terminology, 'babbies, mirrors, the dark, Jenny Marx as the "mad-woman" in the living room'. He has managed a formal dramatic strategy within which to contain feminist ideology. Most effectively of all, he has populated his plays with powerful characters, such as Rebecca, Greta, Mary, Lizzie, Pyper, Michael and Edward, who espouse the feminine principle, not as ideological mouthpieces, but as human beings ineluctably driven to it by their circumstances. These plays form an oeuvre that declares that an appreciation of gender issues is necessary to understand the world, and an embracing of the feminine is necessary to survive it less painfully.

McGuinness demonstrates an espousal of feminist principles that is not only 'intentional' (to revert to Kuhn's thesis) but produces a compelling new approach to theatre both North and South, one which will take time to assimilate but whose influence is already obvious in the work of women playwrights and, particularly, in the work of Anne Devlin.

Conclusion

The narrative plot of this book presents an unintentional irony. The form is circular, distinctly unfeminist. But the circle has not closed. Within a small gap of closure rest future possibilities. In Northern Ireland at the beginning of a new millennium an uneasy peace reigns. Loyalist murders loyalist and republicans maraud with baseball bats. Violence has turned inward, not so much the wolf consuming itself as the cubs devouring each other while the beast sleeps in a little world of its own. If these are the final vestiges of 'the war on the streets', then 'the war in the heads' suggests a more prolonged business of anger and harrowing psychological loss, as well as hope for a better future. In the writing of theatre, these expositions lie within the orbit of the women playwrights who have already established forms within which to address metaphorical and, perhaps, real solutions. Frank McGuinness has consistently espoused a feminist form of non-closure to advocate new mores for new societies. Christina Reid looks back and forward to express homage and discontent alike.

Within a new political language of pluralism and inclusivity in Northern Ireland, our contemporary playwrights have foreseen the need for strategies and have introduced a concomitant language of implementation. This has not always been appreciated or understood by critics and perhaps a new language of criticism is as important as the new language and forms our playwrights are moulding.

Reverting to an article written in 1987 and purporting to 'excavate' old forms of Ulster theatre while criticising output, Philomena Muinzer was to demonstrate how plays about Ulster 'share a body of themes which become part of an inherited dramatic fabric, which then prejudices new political analysis and new creative thinking alike'. Playwrights from Northern Ireland were accused of doing 'little to analyze the events, let alone to suggest a resolution of a crisis which is coming to be accepted as somehow endemic and inevitable'.[1] This article did nothing to describe 'an inherited dramatic fabric' and less to highlight how 'new political analysis and creative thinking' are 'prejudiced'. Textual atrocities were, according to Muinzer, evidence of the 'habitual regression of the writers' mind'. Their obsession with the past is described as 'a self-conscious trait'. Assumptions like Muinzer's mirror those of feminist and other critics who seem to expect radical and revolutionary writing from the most conservative outpost of Western society.

The post-colonial hegemony of sectarianism has overshadowed and annihilated an insurrection of socialism, and while feminism and socialism are not interchangeable, and, indeed, historically represent uncomfortable partnerships, in Northern Ireland the impossibility of one has denied the potential of the other. While the ideological possibility of a theatre that interrogates colonial hegemony found substance in the early work of the ULT and its adherence to the values of the Enlightenment, both audience reception and political hegemony, the latter personified and enacted by W.B. Yeats, dictated a new brand of cultural colonialism. The 'citadel' was built to house rather than to challenge, to erect a monument to local values and to obstruct external influences. It worked well. The Moderns, Joyce, Beckett and Synge, were kept at more than arm's length and a filtration of new ideology lasted for almost a century.

The cultural-political terrain of Ulster might have been radically altered if the ULT had not suffered rejection by Yeats. It has taken a century to come full circle to the recognition of political values of equality and pluralism, almost the exact language of 1902 in a contemporary Ulster in a new millennium. The patriarchy which has reigned to obstruct the implementation of these values has been the subject of this book. The work of Frank McGuinness, Anne Devlin, Marie Jones and Christina Reid reinstates the ideology of the ULT in contemporary terms. And while formal exorcisms are still contested by some critics who refute the introduction of new forms to deal with new realities or potentialities, a feminine voice *has* been defining the gender and tenor of solutions to the Northern 'problem'.

When Muinzer complained that drama in Northern Ireland had not provided 'solutions', she was absolutely right. One wonders what 'solutions' she may have had in mind, particularly at her distance from the problem. When Sam Thompson in the 1960s presented the horrors of sectarianism as social realism, he changed the face, if not the form, of Ulster theatre. There was no retreating back over that bridge and, at the same time, no form in which to develop dramatic challenges to hegemonies of religion, class and patriarchy. The ideology of the Irish Literary Revival in the South has been well and truly obviated. The epic theatre of Bertolt Brecht never took root in Ireland, North or South, resulting in a void of form that had to be addressed.

Solutions that may not exist in real life become metaphors for Devlin, Jones, Reid and McGuinness. They depend on new forms and expositions within their work. These playwrights create and re-create societies within societies, communities which are ostracised and individuals who are long past the accepted norms of social endurance. They pioneer imaginative territories to invent spaces that are distanced from the here and now of naturalism. They create possibilities of 'solutions'. McGuinness's meta-communities in *Observe the Sons of Ulster Marching Towards the Somme, Carthaginians, Someone Who'll Watch Over Me*; Devlin's disparate sisters in *After Easter*; Reid's female exiles, for whom life is not much happier but more authentic – Beth and Theresa in *Tea in a China Cup*, Andrea in *My Name, Shall I Tell You My Name . . . ?*, Sandra in *Clowns*; and Jones's social itinerants in *A Night in November, Hang All the Harpers, Women on the Verge of HRT* and *Stones in His Pockets* all seek and find new lives, while the texts prescribe new life for Northern Ireland.

The potential of a new society is matched by the creation of new dramatic forms. These are open-ended, metaphysical, stretching the psychic journeys of characters and audience alike. The form seems essential to the absorption and transcendence of tragedy moving beyond its literal representation. The social representation of women, either as victims or as isolated matriarchs, is matched by the naturalism of the Ulster genre.

Both McGuinness in *The Factory Girls* and Devlin in *Ourselves Alone* are bound by the form. They cannot shift their female characters beyond the masculine boundaries imposed on them. Both texts make feminist statements in their exposition of patriarchy but the naturalistic form and, indeed, the socio-political reality it represents prevent the formal openness of the feminist text. Like Reid's literal emigrations towards freedom, McGuinness shifts his characters out of their familiar environments to achieve psychic liberation within a freer, open feminine form. *Mary and Lizzie* exemplifies the feminist form in the duo's open-ended journey. Devlin strives towards the feminist form by combining psychological journeys with positive references to English literature and culture. She and Reid represent the patriarchy of republican and loyalist 'freedom' fighters, within which there can be no liberation for women.

Like McGuinness in *Carthaginians*, Devlin images a psychic freedom that involves for Greta (*After Easter*) an exorcism of the past, and future public and private regeneration. Similarly, Reid, in *Clowns*, inhales the breathless antics of the day-to-day, which disguise unresolved legacies of personal and public grief, which must be faced by her characters and Northern Ireland alike. The form of naturalism is at once endorsed and inverted. Jones adopts a style of Ulster comedy to invent a new comic form within which stereotypes are not just presented, but interrogated. A struggle with new forms unites these playwrights as much as the subject matter they share.

The similarities between *Carthaginians* and *After Easter* highlight the movement forward in Ulster theatre. Both illustrate the limitations of naturalism. *Carthaginians'* 'The Burning Balaclava' and *After Easter*'s literalism of language ascribed to Rose and Aoife relate back to earlier idioms and forms. In so doing, they set in motion comparisons and demonstrate the necessity of change, of new language and form to describe new ontologies. In both texts, personal resurrections symbolise potential public renewal. The security of the hybrid identities of Manus (*After Easter*) and Dido (*Carthaginians*) provides a fixed point of social comparison and generates gender as the central issue. The narrow ground of Catholicism is criticised and revised within a bigger picture of metaphor and meaning. But more importantly, the finales articulate and underline the form. Dido's leave-taking spells out textual form:

> What happened? Everything happened, nothing happened, whatever you want to believe, I suppose.[2]

And in *After Easter*, Helen, the supreme, self-manufactured, economically successful and socially integrated fake, describes the form of the text:

> I forget for a moment what it is I'm supposed to see and that's when I achieve it. That's when I come closest, when I grasp the possibilities before the walls or the rooms I'm supposed to see assert themselves.[3]

McGuinness underlines diversity of audience reception, while Devlin asserts the necessity of removing given boundaries of perception. Jones enjoys popular success by employing stereotypes to interrogate fixed perceptions of identity and, within her particular comic form, to manage social transformations. Reid highlights the social phenomenon of one generation's icons becoming another's lumber. It is a comprehension of gender as central to the impasse of Northern Ireland that distinguishes and unites these playwrights. They create possibilities by means of more complex theatrical forms.

Within a supposedly post-feminist Europe, as Charabanc stated in the 1980s, 'we don't want to start that sort of war', one which almost twenty years later would be neither fashionable nor credible and perhaps as much of an anachronism as the ideology of the ULT at the beginning of the last century. However, gender in the broadest sense is still a political issue within Northern Ireland and the impact of cultural feminisation will take time. Our playwrights have heralded the need for new forms; they are, in Muinzer's terms, 'evacuating the museum', and, indeed, have demolished the 'citadel'. Now, a new language of criticism is essential to describe and inscribe dramatic forms.

Glossary

Ulster While theatre in Northern Ireland has traditionally been referred to as 'Ulster theatre', the terminology derives from the founding of the Ulster Literary Theatre as a branch of the Irish Literary Theatre (1902). The province of Ulster still comprises nine counties, as it did in pre-partition Ireland, and today three of the counties lie south of the border. I have endorsed this regional distinction because of these traditional associations and as an expedient measure to allow inclusion of the work of Frank McGuinness, from Buncrana, County Donegal – a county outside of Northern Ireland but within Ulster. While recognising that the term 'Ulster' has derived connotations which relate historically to separatism, anti-Home Rule and loyalism, a particularly Protestant hue is matched, as Susan McKay[1] points out, by ideas of politics and power which are 'male' – Ulster as an issue of gender enters the framework.

male, female Biological terms delineating sexual difference (not to be confused with social constructs of difference employed by adjectives 'masculine' and 'feminine').

feminism The definition may refer to the movement of the 1970s which campaigned to attain equal rights for women. While seen as political doctrine at that time, current usage implies an ideological shift whereby feminine values are asserted to create positive social transformation. A style or ideology that is anti-autocracy and anti-patriarchal is my defining guideline. I employ the term mostly in Chapter 6 to indicate a clear stance against male oligarchy, and in Chapter 3, where an analysis of Charabanc Theatre Company identifies a localised political fear of gendered terminology.

feminist criticism Feminist critical theory, particularly in Chapter 6, is employed to debate issues such as the male 'appropriation' of the feminine versus the capability of the male to produce feminine work. Theorists Annette Kuhn, Toril Moi and others are pitted against Declan Kiberd, and the argument that feminist writing is the inheritance of the Moderns is debated.

feminine The adjective has traditional connotations relating to polite, passive behaviour of the female in support of the male. I employ the term in a positive sense, insinuating values relating to the female – openness of emotional expression and understanding. In this work the feminine male has absorbed some of the values of female and subverts dominant culture. The term 'feminine' does not imply a particular sexual orientation.

masculine Traditionally the term relates to a superior physique, to power, control and authority, responsibility for a weaker sex and offspring. I use it to criticise such dominance and interrogate a binary culture which prevents pluralism, inclusion and cross-fertilisation of ideologies.

patriarchy 'A system of male authority which oppresses women through its social, political and economic institutions. In any of the historical forms that patriarchal society takes, whether it is feudal, capitalist or socialist, a sex/

gender system and a system of economic discrimination operate simultaneously. Patriarchy has power from men's greater access to, and mediation of, the resources and rewards of authority structures inside and outside the home.'[2] The term must be distinct from 'masculinity', 'masculine' and 'male' – terms which do not necessarily imply female oppression.

gender The term 'gender' is not based on biological facts of sex but is a cultural phenomenon of attributes and behaviours given to the male or female. As with corollary terminology, 'feminine', 'masculine', 'patriarchy', etc., I employ the term in its broadest sense in relation to all aspects of culture. In particular, the state of Northern Ireland is repeatedly referred to as 'masculine', not simply because of the literal exclusion of women from public life, but because of hegemonies relating to all aspects of Northern society.

Select Bibliography

PRIMARY TEXTS

Boyd, John. *The Flats*, Belfast, Blackstaff Press, 1973

Devlin, Anne. *Ourselves Alone*, London, Faber and Faber, 1986
— *After Easter*, London, Faber and Faber, 1994

Ervine, St John. *Mixed Marriage,* in *Selected Plays of St John Ervine,*
chosen and edited by John Cronin, Gerrards Cross, Colin Smythe,
1988

Friel, Brian. *Selected Plays*, London, Faber and Faber, 1984

Heaney, Seamus. *North*, London, Faber and Faber, 1975
— *Station Island*, London, Faber and Faber, 1984
— *Sweeney Astray: A Version from the Irish*, New York, Farrar, Straus and
Giroux, 1985

Jones, Marie. *Weddins, Weeins and Wakes*, unpublished texts, June 1989 and
     July 2001
— *Women on the Verge of* HRT, London, Samuel French, 1999
— *A Night in November*, London, Nick Hern Books, 2000
— *Stones in His Pockets*, London, Nick Hern Books, 2000
Jones, Marie, with Charabanc Theatre Company. *Gold in the Streets*,
     unpublished text, 1985
— *Now You're Talking'*, unpublished text, 1985
— *The Girls in the Big Picture*, unpublished text, 1986
— *Somewhere Over the Balcony,* unpublished text, 1987
Jones, Marie and Shane Connaughton. *Hang All the Harpers*, unpublished
     text, 1991
McGuinness, Frank. *The Factory Girls*, Dublin, Monarch Line Press, 1982
— *Observe the Sons of Ulster Marching Towards the Somme*, London, Faber and
     Faber, 1986
— *Carthaginians and Baglady*, London, Faber and Faber, 1988
— *Caoin*, Ulster Youth Theatre, 1989, Linen Hall Library, Theatre and
     Performing Arts Archive
— *Mary and Lizzie*, London, Faber and Faber, 1989
— *Someone Who'll Watch Over Me*, London, Faber and Faber, 1992
— *Frank McGuinness*: *Plays 1*, London, Faber and Faber, 1996
MacNamara, Gerald. *Thompson in Tir na nÓg*, Dublin, Talbot Press,
     1912
— *The Mist that Does Be on the Bog, Suzanne and the Sovereigns, Thompson on
     Terra Firma*, in ed. Kathleen Danaher, *Journal of Irish Literature*,
     vol. 17, nos 2 and 3 (May–September 1988)
Milligan, Alice. *The Last Feast of the Fianna, A Dramatic Legend*, London, David
     Nutt, 1900
— *The Daughter of Donagh, A Cromwellian Drama in Four Acts*, Dublin,
     Martin Lester, 1920
— *Oisin in Tir na nÓg*, Dublin, Gill and Macmillan, 1944
Reid, Christina. *Plays: 1*, London, Methuen Publishing Limited, 1997
     (includes *Tea in a China Cup, Did You Hear the One About the
     Irishman . . . ?, Joyriders, The Belle of the Belfast City, My Name, Shall I
     Tell You My Name?, Clowns*). For permission to perform these

plays, apply to Alan Brodie Representation Ltd, 211 Piccadilly, London W1J 9HF (www.alanbrodie.com)

— *The King of the Castle*, unpublished text, 1999; published text, *New Plays for Young People*, New Connections, London, Faber and Faber, 1999

Synge, J.M. *John Millington Synge: Plays*, ed. Ann Saddlemyer, London, Oxford University Press, 1969

— *Riders to the Sea*, in ed. John P. Harrington, *Modern Irish Drama*, New York and London, W.W. Norton, 1991

Thompson, Sam. *Over the Bridge*, Introduction by Stewart Parker, Dublin, Gill and Macmillan, 1970

Yeats, W.B. *Cathleen Ni Houlihan*, in ed. John P. Harrington, *Modern Irish Drama*, New York and London, W.W. Norton, 1991

SECONDARY SOURCES AND RELATED TEXTS

Agreement, The, Belfast, Northern Ireland Office, 1998

Bardon, Jonathan. *A History of Ulster*, 2nd edn, Belfast, Blackstaff Press, 2001

Barnes, Clive. 'Keeping Up with Jones', *New York Post*, 2 April 2001

Baym, Nina. 'The Madwoman and Her Languages', in eds Robyn R. Warhol and Diane Price Herndl, *Feminisms: An Anthology of Literary Theory and Criticism*, New Brunswick, Rutgers University Press, 1991

Bell, Desmond. *Acts of Union: Sectarianism and Youth Culture in Northern Ireland*, Basingstoke, Macmillan Educational, 1990

Bell, Sam Hanna. 'A Banderol', in ed. David Kennedy, *The Arts in Ulster*, London, George C. Harrap, 1951, pp. 14–15

— *The Theatre in Ulster*, Dublin, Gill and Macmillan, 1972

Billington, Michael. 'Someone Who'll Watch Over Me', *Guardian*, 13 July 1992

Brantley, Ben. 'Wearing Everyone's Shoes, Yet Being Themselves', *New York Times*, 2 April 2001

Buckley, Suzanne and Pamela Lonergan. 'Women and the Troubles 1969–1980', in eds Yonah Alexander and Alan O'Day, *Terrorism in Ireland*, London, Croom Helm; New York, St Martin's Press, 1984

Byrne, Ophelia. *The Stage in Ulster from the Eighteenth Century*, Belfast, Linen Hall Library, 1997

Case, Sue-Ellen. *Feminism and Theatre*, Basingstoke, Macmillan, 1988

Cave, Richard Allen. 'J'accuse', *Theatre Ireland*, no. 21 (1989), pp. 58–62

Chesler, Phyllis. *Women and Madness*, New York, Doubleday, 1972

Colgan, Gerry. 'Carthaginians in Galway', *Irish Times*, 7 February 1992

Coveney, Michael. 'Armalite and the Man', *Financial Times*, 8 October 1988
    — 'Possession as Nine-Tenths of Love', *Observer*, 19 July 1992

Coyle, Jane. 'Carthaginians Makes an Impact on Derry', *Irish Times*,
        14 March 1992
    — 'Curtain Call', *Omnibus* (spring 1993), pp. 24–5

Danaher, Kathleen. 'Introduction to the Plays of Gerald MacNamara',
        Journal of Irish Literature, vol. 17, nos 2 and 3 (May–September 1988)

Davis, Tracy C. 'Extremities and Masterpieces: A Feminist Paradigm of Art
        and Politics', *Modern Drama*, vol. 32, no. 1 (March 1989), p. 96

Dawe, Gerald and Edna Longley (eds). *Across a Roaring Hill: The Protestant
        Imagination in Modern Ireland*, Belfast, Blackstaff Press, 1985

Devlin, Paddy. 'First Bridge too Far', *Theatre Ireland*, no. 3 (1982), pp. 122–4

DiCenzo, Maria R. 'Charabanc Theatre Company: Placing Women Center-
        Stage in Northern Ireland', *Theatre Journal*, no. 45 (1993), pp. 173–84

Eagleton, Terry. *Nationalism, Colonialism and Literature*, Field Day Pamphlet,
        no. 13, Derry, Field Day, 1988

Edgerton, Lynda. 'Public Protest, Domestic Acquiescence: Women in
        Northern Ireland', in eds Rosemary Ridd and Helen Calloway, *Caught
        Up in Conflict*, London, Macmillan Press, 1985

Elliott, Marianne. *Watchmen in Sion: The Protestant Idea of Liberty*, Field Day
        Pamphlet, no. 8, Derry, Field Day, 1985

Ellis-Fermor, Una. *The Irish Dramatic Movement*, London, Methuen,
        1939, 1954

Erlanger, Steven. 'Staging a Little History', *Boston Globe*, 14 February 1986

Evason, Eileen. *Hidden Violence*, Belfast, Farset Co-op Press, 1982
    — *Against the Grain: The Contemporary Women's Movement in Northern
    Ireland*, Dublin, Attic Press, 1991

Fearon, Kate. *Women's Work: The Story of the Northern Ireland Women's
        Coalition*, Belfast, Blackstaff Press, 1999

Finegan, John. 'Derry Air Waiting for a Miracle', *Evening Herald*,
        27 September 1988

Fisk, Robert. 'Out of that Darkness,' *Independent on Sunday*, 27 September 1992

Foley, Imelda. 'History's Moral Guardians Alerted', *Fortnight*, no. 305 (April 1992), pp. 36–7

Grant, David. 'Salt in the Ashes', *Independent*, 28 September 1988

Gregory, Augusta (Lady). 'Our Irish Theatre', in ed. John P. Harrington, *Modern Irish Drama*, New York and London, W.W. Norton, 1991

Griffith, Arthur. *United Irishman*, 10 and 17 October 1903

Hackett, Claire. 'Self-determinism: The Republican Feminist Agenda', *Feminist Review*, no. 50 (summer 1995)

Harris, Claudia W. 'Reinventing Women: Charabanc Theatre Company; Recasting Northern Ireland's Story', in ed. Eberhard Bort, *The State of Play: Irish Theatre in the 'Nineties*, Trier, Wissenschaftlicher Verlag, 1996

Headrick, Charlotte J. 'A Time to Heal: Women Playwrights on the Troubles', unpublished paper for American/Canada Association for Irish Studies Conference, Belfast, 27 June 1995

Hewitt, John. 'Writing in Ulster', *The Bell*, vol. 18, no. 4 (1952), pp. 197–203

Hill, Myrtle and Vivienne Pollock. *Image and Experience, Photographs of Irishwomen c. 1880–1920*, Belfast, Blackstaff Press, 1993

Hoey, Cavan. 'Observe the Sons of Ulster Marching Towards the Somme', *Theatre Ireland*, nos 9 and 10 (December–March 1985), p. 141

Hogan, Robert. *After the Irish Renaissance: A Critical History of Irish Drama*, Minneapolis, University of Minnesota Press, 1967

— *The Macmillan Dictionary of Irish Literature*, London, Macmillan, 1980

Hogan, R. and J. Kilroy. *The Irish Literary Theatre 1899–1901*, Dublin, Dolmen Press, 1975

Hosey, Seamus. 'Carthaginians', *Sunday Tribune*, 2 October 1988

Hughes, Eamon. *Culture and Politics in Northern Ireland*, Milton Keynes, Open University Press, 1991

Humm, Maggie (ed.). *Feminisms: A Reader*, Hemel Hemstead, Harvester Wheatsheaf, 1992

Jardine, Alice. 'Introduction to Julia Kristeva's Women's Time', *Signs*, vol. 7, no. 1 (autumn 1981), pp. 5–12

Johnson, Toni O'Brien and David Cairns (eds). *Gender in Irish Writing*, Milton Keynes, Open University Press, 1991

Johnston, Sheila Turner. *Alice: A Life of Alice Milligan*, Omagh, Colourpoint Press, 1994

Jordan, Eamonn. *The Feast of Famine: The Plays of Frank McGuinness*, Bern, Peter Lang, 1997

Kearney, Richard. 'Myth and Terror', *Crane Bag*, vol. 12, no. 1 (1978), pp. 125–39

Keenan, Brian. 'Out of the Shadows', *Irish Times*, 8 May 1993

Kennedy, David. 'The Ulster Region and the Theatre', *Lagan*, Belfast, Lagan Press, 1946

— 'The Drama in Ulster', in *The Arts in Ulster*, London, George C. Harrap, 1951

Kern, Edith. *The Absolute Comic*, New York, Columbia University Press, 1980

Kiberd, Declan. 'Inventing Irelands', *Crane Bag*, vol. 11, no. 1 (1978)

— *Men and Feminism in Modern Literature*, London, Macmillan Press, 1985

— 'Insecurity, Local Piety and Ulsterisation', *Fortnight* (21 October 1995), pp. 11–22

— *Inventing Ireland: The Literature of the Modern Nation*, London, Vintage, 1996

Kristeva, Julia. 'Women's Time', in eds Robyn R. Warhol and Diane Price Herndl, *Feminisms: An Anthology of Literary Theory and Criticism*, New Brunswick, Rutgers University Press, 1991

Kuhn, Annette. *Women's Pictures: Feminism and Cinema*, London, Pandora Press, 1990

Lee, Joseph. *Ireland 1912–1985, Politics and Society*, Cambridge, Cambridge University Press, 1989

Lojek, Helen. 'Myth and Bonding in Frank McGuinness's Observe the Sons of Ulster Marching Towards the Somme', *Canadian Journal of Irish Studies*, vol. 14 (July 1988), pp. 45–53

— 'Difference without Indifference: The Drama of Frank McGuinness and Anne Devlin', *Eire Ireland*, vol. 25 (1990), pp. 56–68

— 'Playing Politics with Belfast's Charabanc Theatre Company', in eds John P. Harrington and Elizabeth J. Mitchell, *Politics and Performance in Contemporary Northern Ireland*, Amherst, University of Massachusetts Press, 1999

Lyons, F.S.L. *Culture and Anarchy in Ireland, 1890–1939*, Oxford, Oxford
        University Press, 1979

McCartney, R.L. *Liberty and Authority in Ireland*, Field Day Pamphlet, no.9,
        Derry, Field Day, 1985

McGuinness, Frank. 'Popular Theatre?', *Crane Bag*, vol. 8, no. 2 (1984),
        p. 109

McGurk, Brendan. 'Commitment and Risk in Anne Devlin's Ourselves
        Alone and After Easter', in ed. Eberhard Bort, *The State of Play: Irish
        Theatre in the 'Nineties*, Trier, Wissenschaftlicher Verlag, 1996

McHenry, Margaret. 'The Ulster Theatre in Ireland', unpublished thesis,
        University of Pennsylvania, 1931, copy held in Linen Hall Library,
        Belfast

McKay, Susan. *Northern Protestants: An Unsettled People*, Belfast, Blackstaff
        Press, 2000

McMullan, Anna. 'Irish Women Playwrights since 1958', in eds Trevor
        R. Griffiths and Margaret Llewellyn-Jones, *British and Irish
        Women Dramatists since 1958*, Buckingham, Open University
        Press, 1993

McWilliams, Monica. 'Women in Northern Ireland: An Overview', in ed.
        Eamon Hughes, *Culture and Politics in Northern Ireland*, Milton Keynes,
        Open University Press, 1991

Marriott, Sarah. 'Turning Violence on the Family', *Irish Times*, 30 July
        1998

Martin, Carol. 'Charabanc Theatre Company: "Quare" Women "Sleggin"
        and "Geggin" the Standards of Northern Ireland by "Tappin" the
        People', *Toulane Drama Review* (June 1986), p. 97

Maxwell, D.E.S. *A Critical History of Modern Irish Drama 1891–1980*,
        Cambridge, Cambridge University Press, 1984

— 'Northern Ireland's Political Drama', *Modern Drama*, vol. 33, no. 1
        (March 1990), pp. 1–13

Mayne, Rutherford. 'The Plays of Gerald MacNamara', *Dublin Magazine*,
        no. 13 (1938), pp. 53–6

— 'The Ulster Literary Theatre', *Dublin Magazine*, vol. 31 (1955),
        pp. 15–21

Mengel, Hagel. 'A Lost Heritage', *Theatre Ireland*, nos 1 and 2 (1982), p. 18

Mhic Sheain, Brighid. 'Glimpses of Erin', *Fortnight*, Supplement
    (3 September 1971), p. 23

Milligan, Alice. *Shan Van Vocht*, issue 1, vol. 1 (January 1896)

Mitchell, Juliet. *Psychoanalysis and Feminism*, London, Penguin Books, 1974
    — 'What is Feminism?', in eds Juliet Mitchell and Annie Oakley,
        Reflections on Twenty Years of Feminism, Oxford, Basil Blackwell, 1986

Moi, Toril. *Sexual/Textual Politics: Feminist Literary Theory*, London and New
    York, Methuen, 1985

Muinzer, Philomena. 'Evacuating the Museum: The Crisis of Playwriting in
    Ulster', *New Theatre Quarterly*, vol. 3, no. 9 (1987), pp. 44–63

Murray, Christopher. 'Recent Irish Drama', in ed. Heinz Kosok, *Studies in
    Anglo-Irish Literature*, Bouvier, Bonn, 1982
    — *Twentieth-Century Irish Drama: Mirror Up to a Nation*, Manchester,
        Manchester University Press, 1997

Northern Ireland Women's Coalition. *Common Cause: The Story of the
    Northern Ireland Women's Coalition*, Belfast, NIWC, 1998

Nowlan, David. 'Observe the Sons of Ulster Marching Towards the Somme
    at the Peacock', *Irish Times*, 19 February 1985
    — 'Carthaginians at the Peacock', *Irish Times*, 29 September 1988
    — 'Theatre at Its Most Riveting', *Irish Times*, 13 February 1997

O'Connor, Joseph. 'Theatre', *Magill*, 7 March 1985

O'Hehir, Kathryn. 'Alice Milligan: The Celtic Twilight's Forgotten Star',
    unpublished MA thesis submitted to University of North Dakota, May
    1991, now held in Omagh Library

Orr, Philip. *The Road to the Somme: Men of the Ulster Division Tell Their Story*,
    Belfast, Blackstaff Press, 1982

O'Toole, Fintan. 'The Peacock Parade', *Theatre Ireland*, no. 2 (1982), p. 70
    — 'Doomed Dreams of Decency', *Irish Times*, 11 February 1997

Pascal, Julia. 'Is It Feminist?', *City Limits*, 4 September 1986

Penny, Liz. 'In the Forbidden City', *Theatre Ireland*, no. 12 (1987), p. 62

Peter, John. 'Theatre', *Sunday Times*, 2 October 1988

Radcliffe, Michael. 'Passion in Public', *Observer*, 9 October 1988

Reid, Forrest. 'Eighteen Years' Work', *Times Irish Supplement*, 5 December
    1922

Reynolds, W.B. *Uladh*, no. 1, parts 1 and 2 (November 1904), p. 18

Roche, Anthony. *Contemporary Irish Drama from Beckett to McGuinness*, Dublin, Gill and Macmillan, 1994

Saddlemyer, Ann (ed.). *The Collected Letters of J.M. Synge*, vol. 1, 1871–1907, Oxford, Clarendon Press, 1983

Shannon, Catherine B. 'Catholic Women and the Northern Irish Troubles', in eds Yonah Alexander and Alan O' Day, *Ireland's Terrorist Trauma*, New York and London, Harvester Wheatsheaf, 1989

— 'Women in Northern Ireland', in eds Mary O'Dowd and Sabine Wichert, *Chattel, Servant or Citizen: Women's Status in Church, State and Society*, Historical Studies 19, Belfast, Institute of Irish Studies, Queen's University Belfast, 1995

— 'The Woman Writer as Historical Witness: Northern Ireland, 1968–1994, An Interdisciplinary Perspective', in eds Mary Ann Gialanella and Mary O'Dowd, *Women and Irish History*, Dublin, Wolfhound Press, 1997

Thurber, Robin. 'Triumph of the Word', *Guardian*, 10 October 1988

Walker, Lynda. *Godmothers and Mentors, Politics and Education in Northern Ireland*, published dissertation, Belfast, School of Education, Queen's University Belfast, 1996

Ward, Margaret. *Unmanageable Revolutionaries: Women and Irish Nationalism*, London, Pluto Press, 1983

Welch, Robert (ed.). *The Oxford Companion to Irish Literature*, Oxford, Clarendon Press, 1996

White, Victoria. 'Towards Post-Feminism?', *Theatre Ireland*, no. 18 (April–June 1989), pp. 33–5

— 'Cathleen Ni Houlihan is not a Playwright', *Theatre Ireland*, no. 30 (winter 1993), pp. 26–9

Wilcox, Angela. 'The Temple of the Lord is Ransacked', *Theatre Ireland*, no. 8 (1984), pp. 87–9

— 'The Memory of Wounds', *Theatre Ireland*, no. 16 (September–November 1988), pp. 6–8

Wilmer, Stephen. 'Women's Theatre in Ireland', *New Theatre Quarterly*, vol. 7 (28 November 1991), p. 358

— 'Beyond National Theatre', *Irish Stage and Screen*, vol. 4, no. 3 (April–May 1992), pp. 13–14

Notes

INTRODUCTION

1 Seamus Heaney, *North*, London, Faber and Faber, 1975.
2 *The Girls in the Big Picture* is the title of Marie Jones's play with Charabanc, first produced in 1986.
3 Monica McWilliams (Northern Ireland Women's Coalition), personal communication.
4 This book represents part one of a larger project to analyse the work of Northern Ireland's independent theatre companies and that of the community drama movement. Every attempt has been made to reduce academic theory and to make this work accessible to students of drama everywhere and to all who enjoy theatre.

CHAPTER 1

1 Ophelia Byrne, *The Stage in Ulster from the Eighteenth Century*, Belfast, Linen Hall Library, 1997, p. 22.
2 *Ibid.*; Lady Gregory, 'Our Irish Theatre', in ed. John P. Harrington, *Modern Irish Drama*, New York and London, W.W. Norton, 1991, p. 378.
3 Letter from Bulmer Hobson to Sam Hanna Bell, quoted by Sam Hanna Bell in *The Theatre in Ulster*, Dublin, Gill and Macmillan, 1972, pp. 1–2.
4 Rutherford Mayne, 'The Ulster Literary Theatre', *Dublin Magazine*, vol. 31 (1955), pp. 15–21; Margaret McHenry, 'The Ulster Theatre in Ireland', unpublished thesis, University of Pennsylvania, 1931.
5 Bell, *The Theatre in Ulster*, p. 4.
6 W.B. Reynolds, editorial, *Uladh*, no.1 (November 1904), part 1 and 2.
7 Editorial, *Uladh*, no. 2 (February 1905).
8 Liam de Paor quoted in Gerald Dawe and Edna Longley (eds), *Across a Roaring Hill: The Protestant Imagination in Modern Ireland*, Belfast, Blackstaff Press, 1985, Introduction.
9 David Kennedy, 'The Drama in Ulster', in *The Arts in Ulster*, London, George C. Harrap, 1951, p. 51.
10 Sam Hanna Bell, 'A Banderol', in *The Arts in Ulster*, pp. 14–15.
11 *Ibid.*
12 Gerald MacNamara, *Suzanne and the Sovereigns*, 1907; *The Mist that Does Be on the Bog*, 1909; *Thompson in Tir na nÓg*, 1912; *The Throwbacks*, 1917; *Fee Faw Fum*, 1923; *No Surrender*, 1928; *Who Fears to Speak*, 1929; *Thompson on Terra Firma*, 1934.
13 MacNamara, *Thompson in Tir na nÓg*, Dublin, Talbot Press, 1912, p. 81.
14 Bell, *Theatre in Ulster*, p. 43.
15 Mayne, 'The Plays of Gerald MacNamara', *Dublin Magazine*, no. 13 (1938), pp. 53–6.
16 Mayne, *Enter Rabbie John*, BBC NI, November 1954.
17 Richard Kearney, 'Myth and Terror', *Crane Bag*, vol. 12, no. 1 (1978), pp. 125–39.
18 MacNamara, *The Mist that Does Be on the Bog*, in ed. Kathleen Danaher, *Journal of Irish Literature*, vol. 17, nos 2 and 3 (May–September 1988), p. 59.
19 *Ibid.*, p. 61.
20 J.M. Synge, *The Shadow of the Glen*, in ed. Ann Saddlemyer, *John Millington Synge: Plays*, London, Oxford University Press, 1969, p. 49.
21 Ann Saddlemyer (ed.), *The Collected Letters of J.M. Synge*, vol. 1, 1871–1907, Oxford, Clarendon Press, 1983, p. 106.
22 D.E.S. Maxwell, *A Critical History of Modern*

Irish Drama 1891–1980, Cambridge, Cambridge University Press, 1984, p. 65.

23 Desmond Bell, *Acts of Union: Sectarianism and Youth Culture in Northern Ireland*, Basingstoke, Macmillan Educational, 1990, p. 64.

24 Mayne, 'The Plays of Gerald MacNamara', pp. 18–19.

25 Kennedy, 'The Drama in Ulster', p. 56.

26 Unreferenced quote by Bell, 'A Banderol', pp. 14–15.

27 John Cronin (ed.), Introduction to *Selected Plays of St John Ervine*, Gerrards Cross, Colin Smythe, 1988, p. 13.

28 *Ibid.*, p. 63.

29 *Ibid.*, p. 28.

30 *Ibid.*, p. 19.

31 Kennedy, 'The Drama in Ulster', p. 51.

32 The Group Theatre management rejected the play on the grounds that it 'would offend and affront every section of the public'. For a full account, see Byrne, *The Stage in Ulster*, pp. 46–9.

33 Paddy Devlin. See also, 'First Bridge too Far', *Theatre Ireland*, no. 3 (1982), pp. 122–4.

34 Stewart Parker, Introduction to Sam Thompson, *Over the Bridge*, Dublin, Gill and Macmillan, 1970.

35 Thompson, *Over the Bridge*, p. 114.

36 Maud Gonne granted the rights of *Cathleen Ni Houlihan* to ULT and Maire Quinn performed in it.

37 Myrtle Hill and Vivienne Pollock, *Image and Experience: Photographs of Irishwomen, c. 1880–1920*, Belfast, Blackstaff Press, 1993, p. 7. The author is indebted to the work of Myrtle Hill, Vivienne Pollock and Margaret Ward for analysing the context within which women operated at the beginning of the twentieth century.

38 Margaret Ward, *Unmanageable Revolutionaries: Women and Irish Nationalism*, London, Pluto Press, 1983, p. 1. (For listing of women's organisations see Index, Ward.)

39 *Ibid.*, p. 2.

40 Hill and Pollock, *Image and Experience*, p. 2.

41 *Ibid.* p. 110.

42 Collection held by the Theatre and Performing Arts Archive, Linen Hall Library, Belfast.

43 McHenry, 'The Ulster Theatre in Ireland', p. 78.

44 Brighid Mhic Sheain, 'Glimpses of Erin', *Fortnight*, Supplement (3 September 1971), p. 23.

45 *Northern Patriot* (15 October 1895).

46 *Shan Van Vocht*, issue 1, vol. 1 (January 1896).

47 Sheila Turner Johnston, *Alice: A Life of Alice Milligan*, Omagh, Colourpoint Press, 1994, pp. 44, 66, 67, 89.

48 *The Peasant* (June 1908), quoted by Johnston, *Alice*.

49 Maud Gonne, *A Servant to the Queen*, unreferenced, quoted in Johnston, *Alice*, p. 91.

50 *Irish Review* (July/August 1914).

51 Ward, *Unmanageable Revolutionaries*, and Declan Kiberd, *Inventing Ireland: The Literature of the Modern Nation*, London, Vintage, 1996, pp. 405–6.

52 Terry Eagleton, *Nationalism, Colonialism and Literature*, Field Day Pamphlet, no. 13, Derry, Field Day, 1988, p. 10.

53 Kiberd, *Inventing Ireland*, p. 398.

54 Ward, *Unmanageable Revolutionaries*, p. 249

55 *United Ireland*, 16 December–23 December 1893.

56 Johnston, *Alice*, p. 94.

57 *Daily Express*, 14–21 January 1899. (Milligan refers to a tableau she had staged in Letterkenny the previous summer. Much praised by Arthur Griffith, Yeats had plagiarised Griffith's criticism.)

58 Quoted in Johnston, *Alice*, p.94.

59 Preface to *The Last Feast of the Fianna*, unreferenced quote in Johnston, *Alice*, p. 100.

60 Robert Hogan, *The Macmillan Dictionary of Irish Literature*, London, Macmillan, 1980, p. 447.

61 *Daily Express*.

62 Quoted in Johnston, *Alice*, pp. 101–2.

63 Alice Milligan, *The Daughter of Donagh, A Cromwellian Drama in Four Acts*, Dublin, Martin Lester, 1920, p. 25.

64 Jonathan Bardon, *A History of Ulster*, 2nd edn, Belfast, Blackstaff Press, 2001, p. 424.

65 Johnston, *Alice*, p. 7

66 *Ibid.*

67 Forrest Reid, 'Eighteen Years' Work', *Times Irish Supplement*, 5 December 1922.

68 John Hewitt, 'Writing in Ulster', *The Bell*, vol. 18, no. 4 (1952), p. 200.

69 Byrne, *The Stage in Ulster*, pp. 40–41.

CHAPTER 2

1 Victoria White, 'Cathleen Ni Houlihan is not a Playwright', *Theatre Ireland* (April–June 1989), p. 29.

2 *The Agreement*, Belfast, Northern Ireland Office, 1998. See section 'Safeguards and Equality of Opportunity'.

3 See Anna McMullan, 'Irish Women

Playwrights since 1958', in eds Trevor R. Griffiths and Margaret Llewellyn-Jones, *British and Irish Women Dramatists since 1958*, Buckingham and Philadelphia, Open University Press, 1993, p. 111. See also Catherine B. Shannon, 'Catholic Women and the Northern Irish Troubles', in eds Yonah Alexander and Alan O'Day, *Ireland's Terrorist Trauma*, New York and London, Harvester Wheatsheaf, 1989, p. 235.

4   Lynda Walker, *Godmothers and Mentors: Women, Politics and Education in Northern Ireland*, published dissertation, Belfast, School of Education, Queen's University Belfast, 1996, p. 8.

5   Lynda Edgerton, 'Public Protest, Domestic Acquiescence: Women in Northern Ireland', in eds Rosemary Ridd and Helen Calloway, *Caught Up in Conflict*, London, Macmillan Press, 1985, p. 73.

6   Bernadette Devlin, 'We Want Peace. Just Peace', *New York Times Magazine*, 19 December 1976, p. 30.

7   *Ibid.*, p. 76.

8   Walker, *Godmothers and Mentors*, p. 7.

9   Edgerton, 'Public Protest, Domestic Acquiescence', p. 24.

10   The response of Catholic women to internment and rioting is examined by Catherine B. Shannon in another essay, 'Women in Northern Ireland', in eds Mary O'Dowd and Sabine Wichert, *Chattel, Servant or Citizen: Women's Status in Church, State and Society*, Historical Studies 19, Belfast, Institute of Irish Studies, Queen's University Belfast, 1995, p. 243.

11   Edgerton, 'Public Protest, Domestic Acquiescense', p. 19.

12   Introduction, *Common Cause: The Story of the Northern Ireland Women's Coalition*, NIWC pamphlet, 1998. See also Kate Fearon, *Women's Work: The Story of the Northern Ireland Women's Coalition*, Belfast, Blackstaff Press, 1999.

13   *Ibid.*

14   Suzanne Buckley and Pamela Lonergan, 'Women and the Troubles 1969–1980', in eds Alan O'Day and Yonah Alexander, *Terrorism in Ireland*, London, Croom Helm; New York, St Martin's Press, 1984, p. 86.

15   Edgerton, 'Public Protest, Domestic Acquiescence', p. 82.

16   *Ibid.* Long Kesh was an airfield during the Second World War and in the early 1970s the Nissen huts were utilised as an internment camp, later to become the site of the Maze Prison.

CHAPTER 3

1   Carol Martin, 'Charabanc Theatre Company: "Quare" Women "Sleggin" and "Geggin" the Standards of Northern Ireland by "Tappin" the People', *Toulane Drama Review* (June 1986), p. 97.

2   Charabanc Theatre Company, Statement of Policy, 1983, Theatre and Performing Arts Archive, Linen Hall Library, Belfast.

3   Jane Coyle, 'Curtain Call', *Omnibus* (spring 1993), p. 24.

4   Marie Jones, with Charabanc Theatre Company, unpublished text, *The Girls in the Big Picture*, 1986.

5   Field Day Theatre Company was founded by Brian Friel and Stephen Rea in 1981, two years before the foundation of Charabanc.

6   Helen Lojek, 'Playing Politics with Belfast Charabanc Theatre Company', in eds John P. Harrington and Elizabeth J. Mitchell, *Politics and Performance in Contemporary Northern Ireland*, Amherst, University of Massachusetts Press, 1999, pp. 82–90. See also Maria R. DiCenzo's article 'Charabanc Theatre Company: Placing Women Center-stage in Northern Ireland', *Theatre Journal*, no. 45 (1993), pp. 173–84. Both Lojek and DiCenzo emphasise the all-male board of Field Day.

7   Transcript of panel discussion, *Is Ireland a Matriarchy or Not? The Experience of Irish Women as Theatre Artist*, International Arts Conference for the Study of Irish Literature, Belfast, June 1995, moderated by Claudia W. Harris and quoted by her in 'Reinventing Women: Charabanc Theatre Company; Recasting Northern Ireland's Story', in ed. Eberhard Bort, *The State of Play: Irish Theatre in the 'Nineties*, Trier, Wissenschaftlicher Verlag, 1996, p. 114.

8   Lojek, 'Playing Politics', p. 100.

9   Brian Friel, *Selected Plays*, London, Faber and Faber, 1984, p. 427.

10   *The Girls in the Big Picture*, pp. 58–9.

11   See Chapter 1, p. 3.

12   Lojek, 'Playing Politics', p. 95.

13   Martin, 'Charabanc Theatre Company', p. 97.

14   Steven Erlanger, 'Staging a Little History', *Boston Globe*, 14 February 1986.

15   Harris, 'Reinventing Women', p. 115.

16   Christopher Murray, *Twentieth-Century Irish Drama: Mirror Up to a Nation*, Manchester, Manchester University Press, 1997, p. 194.

17   Spelling as in text, p. 68.

18   Marie Jones, with the Charabanc Theatre

Company, *Somewhere Over the Balcony*, unpublished text, 1987, pp. 26–7.

19 *Ibid.*, pp. 32–3.

20 *Ibid.*, p. 34.

21 *Ibid.*

22 Edith Kern, *The Absolute Comic*, New York, Columbia University Press, 1980, p. 43.

23 *Ibid.*

24 On 8 November 1987, eleven people were killed and sixty-three injured, nineteen seriously, when a bomb exploded at the annual commemoration of war victims at the cenotaph in Enniskillen.

25 Marie Jones, *Weddins, Weeins and Wakes*, unpublished text, 2001, p. 33.

26 Until recently only male members of the Orange Lodge marched in the Twelfth of July parade, to celebrate the victory of William of Orange over James II at the Battle of the Boyne in 1690. The women walked on the footpaths alongside the main roads on which the men marched.

27 In the midst of a debacle about political censorship with the Arts Council of Northern Ireland, DubbelJoint's announcement of its founding principles came as a surprise. Pam Brighton stated: 'Our source of inspiration was the fact that no other company was doing nationalist plays.' She is referring back to the founding of the company in 1991. See 'Metro Theatre', *Irish News* (23 July 1999).

28 Marie Jones and Shane Connaughton, *Hang All the Harpers,* unpublished text, 1991.

29 During the Williamite War, the Jacobite forces of James II besieged the city of Derry from 18 April to 31 July 1689; the 105-day ordeal was brought to an end when two ships, laden with food, broke the boom blocking the Foyle estuary.

30 *Hang All the Harpers*, p. 89.

31 *A Night in November* was first produced by DubbelJoint Productions at the West Belfast Festival, Belfast Institute of Further and Higher Education, Whiterock Road, 8 August 1994.

32 Marie Jones, *Women on the Verge of HRT*, London, Samuel French, 1999.

33 *Ibid.*, p. 49.

34 Marie Jones, *Stones in His Pocket*, published text, London, Nick Hern Books, 2000, p. 57.

CHAPTER 4

1 Christina Reid, *Plays: 1*, London, Methuen, 1997.

2 Christina Reid, *The King of the Castle*,

unpublished text, commissioned by the National Theatre for BT Connections, a UK Festival of Youth Drama, performed by Methodist College Drama at the National Theatre, London, 12 July 1999. I have quoted from this text throughout.

3 *Ibid.*, p. 28.

4 Steve McBride interview with Christina Reid, 'Leading Lady', in *Peace by Peace*, 10 February 1984, p. 2.

5 Reid, *The Belle of the Belfast City*, in *Plays: 1*, p. 250.

6 *Ibid.*, p. 199.

7 *Ibid.*, p. 205.

8 *Ibid.*, p. 229.

9 *Ibid.*, p. 244.

10 'Two New Plays from Belfast', *Theatre Ireland*, no. 5 (1984), p. 98.

11 *Clowns* was first performed at The Room, The Orange Tree, Richmond, in March 1996; *Joyriders* was first performed at the Tricycle Theatre, London, in February 1986.

12 Christina Reid, *Clowns*, in *Plays: 1*, p. 289.

13 *Ibid.*, p. 319.

CHAPTER 5

1 Anne Devlin, *Ourselves Alone*, London, Faber and Faber, 1986. First performed at the Liverpool Playhouse Studio, 24 October 1985.

2 Catherine B. Shannon, 'The Woman Writer as Historical Witness: Northern Ireland, 1968–1994, An Interdisciplinary Perspective', in eds Mary Ann Gialanella and Mary O'Dowd, *Women and Irish History*, Dublin, Wolfhound Press, 1997, p. 244.

3 In their campaign for the restoration of special category status, republican prisoners in Long Kesh commenced a hunger strike in March 1981, led by Bobby Sands, the Provisional IRA's Officer Commanding in the prison. Ten men died before the protest ended. Sands, who had been elected MP for Fermanagh–South Tyrone, died after sixty-six days of hunger strike.

4 'Sticky' is a colloquial term for the political grouping which severed links with IRA militarism and became the Workers' Party.

5 *Ourselves Alone*, p. 14.

6 *Ibid.*, pp. 13–14.

7 *Ibid.*, p. 18.

8 *Ibid.*, p. 36.

9 The Easter Rising in April 1916 was led by Patrick Pearse and James Connolly, who

took over the General Post Office in Dublin
and demanded freedom from British Rule
and an Irish Republic. On surrender, fifteen
leaders of the rising were executed,
including Pearse and Connolly, and were
subsequently hailed as martyrs.

10   *Ourselves Alone*, p. 39.
11   *Ibid.*
12   *Ibid.*, p. 29.
13   Brendan McGurk, 'Commitment and Risk
      in Anne Devlin's *Ourselves Alone* and *After
      Easter*', in ed. Bort, *The State of Play: Irish
      Theatre in the 'Nineties*, p. 55.
14   *Ourselves Alone*, p. 39.
15   McGurk, 'Commitment and Risk', p. 54.
16   *Ourselves Alone*, p. 88.
17   *Ibid.*, p. 87.
18   Sinn Féin's policy regarding abortion was
      first mooted in 1984 in relation to the
      referendum in the Republic of Ireland
      (calling for a ban on abortion). The
      Workers' Party campaigned against the
      referendum. In 1986, the Sinn Féin Ard
      Fheis voted by a margin of two votes for a
      pro-choice resolution, which was reversed
      the following year. See Shannon, 'Woman
      Writer as Historical Witness', p. 250.
19   *Ourselves Alone*, p. 19.
20   *Ibid.*, p. 45.
21   Shannon, 'Woman Writer as Historical
      Witness', p. 252.
22   A brick is thrown through the window of
      McDermot's flat. A note states, according to
      Frieda, that 'this is a Protestant street',
      Ourselves Alone, pp. 80–81.
23   *Ibid.*, p. 20.
24   *Ibid.*, p. 24.
25   *Ibid.*, p. 31.
26   'Violence against women is doubly difficult
      to report and escape from when it becomes a
      life-threatening act of political disloyalty.'
      As quoted in the Introduction to eds
      Gialanella and O'Dowd, *Women and Irish
      History*, p. 14.
27   Eileen Evason, *Hidden Violence*, Belfast,
      Farset Co-op Press, 1982, p. 73.
28   Angela Courtney quoted by Sarah
      Marriott, 'Turning Violence on the
      Family', *Irish Times*, 30 July 1998, p. 13.
29   *Ibid.*
30   *Ourselves Alone*, p. 41.
31   *Ibid.*, pp. 87–8.
32   *Ibid.*, p. 54.
33   *Ibid.*, p. 39.
34   Anthony Roche, *Contemporary Irish Drama
      from Beckett to McGuinness*, Dublin, Gill and
      Macmillan, 1994, p. 238.
35   *Ourselves Alone*, p. 83.

36   *Ibid.*, p. 53.
37   *Ibid.*, p. 89.
38   *Ibid.*, p. 16.
39   *Ibid.*, p. 90.
40   *Ibid.*, p. 26.
41   *Ibid.*, p. 89.
42   *Ibid.*, p. 80.
43   *Ibid.*, p. 16.
44   *Ibid.*, p. 67.
45   *Ibid.*, p. 65.
46   *Ibid.*, pp. 65–7.
47   Roche, *Contemporary Irish Drama*, p. 238.
48   Helen Lojek, Difference without
      Indifference: The Drama of Frank
      McGuinness and Anne Devlin', *Eire Ireland*,
      vol. 25 (1990), p. 64.
49   Anne Devlin, *After Easter*, London, Faber
      and Faber, 1994, p. 3. First performed by the
      Royal Shakespeare Company, The Other
      Place, Stratford, 18 May 1994, and by the
      Lyric Theatre, Belfast, 3 November 1994.
50   Lojek, 'Difference without Indifference',
      p. 64.
51   Julia Pascal in *City Limits* (4 September
      1986). She asks of *Ourselves Alone*, 'Is it
      feminist? The three women continually
      define themselves through their men.'
      Pascal's abhorrence of such feminist
      deviance, not understanding its relativity, is
      summarised by her final sentence:
      'Overdosing on oestrogen can be bad for a
      woman's health.' Devlin would agree, but
      in this synopsis, text and subtext have
      become confused.
52   Edgerton, 'Public Protest, Domestic
      Acquiescence', p. 61.
53   Shannon, 'Woman Writer as Historical
      Witness', p. 253.
54   *Ibid.*, p. 253.
55   See Claire Hackett, 'Self-determination:
      The Republican Feminist Agenda', *Feminist
      Review*, no. 50 (summer 1995).
56   *Ibid.*, p. 113.
57   *Ibid.*
58   *Ourselves Alone*, p. 21.
59   *Ibid.*, p. 16.
60   Joseph Lee, *Ireland 1912–1985, Politics and
      Society*, Cambridge, Cambridge University
      Press, 1989, p. 652.
61   *After Easter*, p. 4.
62   *Ibid.*, p. 7.
63   These incidents are reported in Greta's
      encounter with Eilish, *After Easter*,
      pp. 21–30.
64   *Ibid.*, p. 16.
65   *Ibid.*, p. 18.
66   *Ibid.*, p. 5.
67   *Ibid.*, p. 8.

68   *Ibid.*, p. 26.
69   *Ibid.*, p. 8.
70   The first scene introduces Greta in a mental hospital recalling her childhood: 'My mother used to scream. She'd run up the stairs after me and pull my hair. She'd shout, "Nobody loves you. Nobody loves you." And I'd think, it doesn't matter because I love me. I don't need anyone.', *ibid.*, p. 1.
71   *Ibid.*, p. 59.
72   Nina Baym, 'The Madwoman and Her Languages', in eds Robyn R. Warhol and Diane Price Herndl, *Feminisms: An Anthology of Literary Theory and Criticism*, New Brunswick, Rutgers University Press, 1991, p. 156.
73   Juliet Mitchell, *Psychoanalysis and Feminism*, London, Penguin Books, 1974, p. 263.
74   Phyllis Chesler, *Women and Madness*, New York, Doubleday, 1972, p. 138.
75   Baym, 'The Madwoman and Her Languages', p. 157. Baym is citing Christiane Makward. For Baym, this description encapsulates the views of those most associated with the idea – Hélène Cixous and Luce Irigaray.
76   *After Easter*, p. 1.
77   *Ibid.*, p. 13.
78   *Ibid.*, p. 66.
79   *Ibid.*, p. 71.
80   *Ibid.*, p. 73.
81   *Ibid.*, p. 75.
82   Seamus Heaney, Introduction, *Sweeney Astray: A Version from the Irish*, cited in Lojek, 'Difference without Indifference', p. 62.
83   Charlotte J. Headrick, 'A Time to Heal: Women Playwrights on the Troubles', unpublished paper, International Arts Conference for the Study of Irish Literature, Belfast, 27 June 1995. Held in the Linen Hall Library.
84   Roche, *Contemporary Irish Drama*, p. 229, and Stephen Wilmer, 'Women's Theatre in Ireland', *New Theatre Quarterly*, vol. 7 (November 1991), p. 358.
85   *Fortnight*, no. 326 (March 1994), p. 38.
86   Reid, *The Belle of the Belfast City*, p. 23.
87   Devlin, *Ourselves Alone*, p. 39.
88   Jones, *Women on the Verge of HRT*, p. 43.
89   Edgerton, 'Public Protest, Domestic Acquiescence', p. 82.

CHAPTER 6

1   The title quotation is from McGuinness in reference to *Carthaginians*. Lecture, Trinity College Dublin, 15 November 1991.
2   Annette Kuhn, *Women's Pictures: Feminism and Cinema*, London, Pandora Press, 1990, p. 9.
3   Declan Kiberd, *Men and Feminism in Modern Literature*, London, Macmillan Press, 1985.
4   Frank McGuinness, 'Popular Theatre?', *Crane Bag*, vol. 8, no. 2 (1984), p. 109.
5   See Chapter 1, which outlines the founding ideology of the ULT.
6   Frank McGuinness, *The Factory Girls*, Dublin, Monarch Line Press, 1982. First performed at the Peacock Theatre, Dublin, in March 1982.
7   Monica McWilliams, 'Women in Northern Ireland: An Overview,' in ed. Eamon Hughes, *Culture and Politics in Northern Ireland*, Milton Keynes, Open University Press, 1991, p. 86.
8   *The Factory Girls*, p. 43.
9   *Ibid.*, p. 44.
10   Eamonn Jordan, *The Feast of Famine: The Plays of Frank McGuinness*, Bern, Peter Lang, 1997, pp. 89–91, 194–6.
11   Fintan O'Toole, 'The Peacock Parade', *Theatre Ireland*, no. 2 (1982), p. 70.
12   Epigraph to *The Factory Girls*.
13   Tracy C. Davis, 'Extremities and Masterpieces: A Feminist Paradigm of Art and Politics', *Modern Drama*, vol. 32, no. 1 (March 1989), p. 96.
14   Seamus Heaney, 'Station Island', *Station Island*, London, Faber and Faber, 1984, pp. 61–94.
15   *Stations* was performed at the Belfast Festival at Queen's, Stranmillis College Theatre, 1989, and at Lombard Street Studio, Dublin, 1990. In 1991, the production was nominated alongside *Dancing at Lughnasa* for the RTÉ/Bank of Ireland Arts Awards, for Best Drama Production of the year.
16   *Caoin* is held in the Ulster Youth Theatre Archive, Linen Hall Library, Belfast. *Stations* was premiered at Stranmillis College Theatre, Belfast, in November 1989.
17   J.M. Synge, *Riders to the Sea*, in ed. John P. Harrington, *Modern Irish Drama*, New York and London, W.W. Norton, 1991.
18   Thirteen Protestant apprentice boys slammed the gates of Derry on the army of Catholic King James II at the start of the 105-day siege of 1689; their action is celebrated annually on 12 August by the Apprentice Boys of Derry. Bloody Sunday: on 30 January 1972 thirteen people were shot dead in Derry by the British Army; a fourteenth died later.

19 Liz Penny, 'In the Forbidden City', *Theatre Ireland*, no. 12 (1987), p. 62.
20 *Ibid.*
21 McGuinness, Trinity College lecture.
22 I refer to the original text except where otherwise stated, *Carthaginians and Baglady*, London, Faber and Faber, 1988. The revised text is published in *Frank McGuinness: Plays 1*, London, Faber and Faber, 1996.
23 *Ibid.*, p. 26.
24 Quotation from Czeslaw Milosz, epigraph, *Carthaginians*: 'It is possible that there is no other memory than the memory of wounds.'
25 *Carthaginians*, p. 7.
26 *Ibid.*, p. 68.
27 *Ibid.*, p. 70.
28 *Ibid.*
29 Joe Dowling, 'New Directions in Irish Theatre', lecture, University College Dublin, 16 November 1991.
30 Michael Coveney, 'Armalite and the Man', *Financial Times*, 8 October 1988.
31 John Finegan, 'Derry Air Waiting for a Miracle', *Evening Herald*, 27 September 1988.
32 David Nowlan, 'Carthaginians at the Peacock', *Irish Times*, 29 September 1988.
33 *Sunday Press*, 2 October 1988.
34 Seamus Hosey, 'Carthaginians', *Sunday Tribune*, 2 October 1988.
35 David Grant, 'Salt in the Ashes', *Independent*, 28 September 1988.
36 Hosey, 'Carthaginians'.
37 Michael Radcliffe, 'Passion in Public', *Observer*, 9 October 1988.
38 John Peter, 'Theatre', *Sunday Times*, 2 October 1988.
39 Robin Thurber, 'Triumph of the Word', *Guardian*, 10 October 1988.
40 Kuhn, *Women's Pictures*, p. 11.
41 *Ibid.*
42 Coveney, 'Armalite and the Man'.
43 Hosey, 'Carthaginians'.
44 Coveney, Armalite and the Man'.
45 See Jane Coyle, 'Carthaginians Makes an Impact on Derry', *Irish Times*, 14 March 1992, and Imelda Foley, 'History's Moral Guardians Alerted', *Fortnight*, no. 305 (April 1992), pp. 36–7, for details of the event, which was not cancelled.
46 Davis, 'Extremities and Masterpieces', p. 96.
47 *Carthaginians*, p. 70.
48 *Ibid*, p. 27.
49 Victoria White, 'Towards Post-Feminism?', *Theatre Ireland*, no. 18 (April–June 1989), pp. 33–4.
50 Juliet Mitchell, 'Psychoanalysis and Feminism' (1974), in ed. Maggie Humm, *Feminisms: A Reader*, Hemel Hemstead, Harvester Wheatsheaf, 1992, p. 239.
51 For analysis of Lacan, see 'From Simone de Beauvoir to Jaques Lacan', in Toril Moi, *Sexual/Textual Politics; Feminist Literary Theory*, London and New York, Methuen, 1985, pp. 99–100.
52 *Ibid.*, p. 135
53 *Ibid.*
54 *Carthaginians*, p. 47.
55 *Ibid.*, p. 16.
56 *Carthaginians*, p. 21.
57 Moi, *Sexual/Textual Politics*, p. 167.
58 Talk by Frank McGuinness for ASPECTS Literature Festival, Bangor, County Down, October 1996.
59 Foley, 'History's Moral Guardians Alerted', p. 36.
60 McGuinness, *Plays 1*, p. 178.
61 Gerry Colgan, 'Carthaginians in Galway', *Irish Times*, 7 February 1992.
62 Jordan, *The Feast of Famine*, p. 91.
63 *Carthaginians*, p. 70.
64 BBC Radio Ulster ran a vox pop on the issue of the National Theatre of Ireland bringing a play about Ulster heritage, written by a Catholic, to Northern Ireland, November 1987.
65 Frank McGuinness, *Mary and Lizzie*, London, Faber and Faber, 1989. First performance at The Pit, Barbican Centre, London, 27 September 1989.
66 Richard Allen Cave, 'J'accuse', *Theatre Ireland*, no. 21 (1989), p. 58.
67 *Ibid.*, p. 60.
68 Alice Jardine, 'Introduction to Julia Kristeva's Women's Time', *Signs*, vol. 7, no. 1 (autumn 1981), pp. 5–12.
69 *Ibid.*
70 Julia Kristeva, 'Women's Time', in eds Warhol and Price Herndl, *Feminisms. An Anthology*, pp. 443–59.
71 *Mary and Lizzie*, p. 1.
72 Frank McGuinness, *Observe the Sons of Ulster Marching Towards the Somme*, London, Faber and Faber, 1986, p. 29.
73 *Ibid.*, p. 33.
74 *Ibid.*, p. 65.
75 David Nowlan, 'Observe the Sons of Ulster Marching Towards the Somme at the Peacock', *Irish Times*, 19 February 1985.
76 Joseph O'Connor, 'Theatre', *Magill*, 7 March 1985.
77 Cavan Hoey, 'Observe the Sons of Ulster Marching Towards the Somme', *Theatre Ireland*, nos 9 and 10 (December–March 1985), p. 141.

78   *Observe the Sons of Ulster*, p. 10.
79   Declan Kiberd, 'Insecurity, Local Piety and Ulsterisation', *Fortnight* (21 October 1995), pp. 11–13.
80   *Observe the Sons of Ulster*, p. 45.
81   Marianne Elliott, *Watchmen in Sion: The Protestant Idea of Liberty*, Field Day Pamphlet, no. 8, Derry, Field Day, 1985.
82   R.L. McCartney, *Liberty and Authority in Ireland*, Field Day Pamphlet, no. 9 Derry, Field Day, 1985, p. 8.
83   *Observe the Sons of Ulster*, p. 12.
84   Helen Lojek, 'Myth and Bonding in Frank McGuinness's "Observe the Sons of Ulster Marching Towards the Somme"', *Canadian Journal of Irish Studies*, vol. 14 (July 1988), pp. 45–53.
85   *Ibid.*
86   *Observe the Sons of Ulster*, p. 10.
87   Philip Orr, Introduction, *The Road to the Somme: Men of the Ulster Division Tell Their Story*, Belfast, Blackstaff Press, 1982, p. 227.
88   *Ibid.*
89   *Observe the Sons of Ulster*, pp. 69–71.
90   McGuinness, Trinity College lecture.
91   Frank McGuinness, *Someone Who'll Watch Over Me*, London, Faber and Faber, 1992. First performed at the Hampstead Theatre, London, July 1992.
92   *Ibid.*, p. 2.
93   *Ibid.*, p. 3.
94   *Ibid.*, p. 10. When the play was performed for one night at the West Belfast Festival, Sunday, 4 August 1992, the audience applauded and laughed at Michael's first line, 'I'm so sorry, but where am I?' (p. 9).
95   *Someone Who'll Watch Over Me*, p. 28.
96   The Marathon workshop was self-contained and although the embryo of a play was created, the final outcome was *Caoin*.
97   *Ibid.*, p. 57.
98   *Ibid.*, p. 58.
99   *Ibid.*, p. 27.
100 Michael Coveney, 'Possession as Nine-Tenths of Love', *Observer*, 19 July 1992.
101 Michael Billington, 'Some Who'll Watch Over Me', *Guardian*, 13 July 1992.
102 Brian Keenan, 'Out of the Shadows', *Irish Times*, 8 May 1993.
103 Frank McGuinness, interview with *Hot Press*, September 1990.
104 In conversation with the author, McGuinness has referred to his appreciation of the French school of feminist thought.

CONCLUSION

1   Philomena Muinzer, 'Evacuating the Museum: The Crisis of Playwriting in Ulster', *New Theatre Quarterly*, vol. 3, no. 9 (1987), pp. 44–63.
2   *Carthaginians*, p. 70.
3   *After Easter*, p. 74.

GLOSSARY

1   Susan McKay, *Northern Protestants: An Unsettled People*, Belfast, Blackstaff Press, 2000, p. 46.
2   Humm, *Feminisms: A Reader*, p. 408.

Index